Don't Come Back Until You Find It

Don't Come Back Until You Find It

TALES FROM
AN
ANTIQUES DEALER

Bruce Newman

B
BEAUFORT BOOKS
NEW YORK

Circ

Copyright © 2006 by Bruce Newman

FIRST EDITION

ISBN 0-8253-0536-5

8

Published in the United States by Beaufort Books, New York
Distributed by Midpoint Trade Book, New Yorks
www.midpointtrade.com

10 9 8 7 6 5 4 3 2 1

PRINTED IN THE UNITED STATES OF AMERICA

6/18/07

$24.95

For Judy, Emily, Nolan, and Phoebe

CONTENTS

Preface   *ix*

Acknowledgments   *xi*

INTRODUCTION   Meeting Jackie   1

PART ONE
From Ellis Island to Newel Art Galleries

CHAPTER ONE   The Immigrant Makes It   19
CHAPTER TWO   The Brighton Pavilion Seals the Deal   35
CHAPTER THREE   Family Interference   49
CHAPTER FOUR   The Fight for Newel   59
CHAPTER FIVE   Taking it to the Top   71

PART TWO
Anecdotes of the Trade

CHAPTER SIX   Barbra, Jane, Sigourney, and McEnroe   89
CHAPTER SEVEN   Dustin, Woody, Rex, and Even Nixon   103

Chapter Eight   The *Normandie* Resurfaces   117
Chapter Nine   Fantasy Furniture   133
Chapter Ten   The Royal Copycat   151

PART THREE
Tips and Tactics

Chapter Eleven   How and Where to Buy   165
Chapter Twelve   Is it Real or Repro?   179
Chapter Thirteen   Clean Up the Act   193
Chapter Fourteen   Reserves, Premiums, and Reforms   205

                     Index   223

Preface

There has been more time fleeting by than I would care to acknowledge. It's been more than four years since I've pounded the sidewalks of London and negotiated the cobblestones of the fleamarkets of Paris, hunting for antiques. Do I miss it? You bet I do! But I guess that's one of the reasons I decided to write this book. So I can keep in touch, by jogging my memory to recall those magical moments of my career. The other reasons are: to give people an idea of how rich and exciting this field can be, to give some practical advice on how and where to buy antiques, to teach the reader to know how to tell the age of antiques, and lastly, to educate the reader about the pitfalls to avoid when dealing with those 800-pound gorillas, the auction houses.

After fifty years in the business, what I don't know about decorative arts could fill the New York Public Library, so if I'm lucky, I will learn a few more things myself—for there's still more out there I want to discover, and I know I can't go home until I've found it.

Acknowledgments

It's impossible to name the many friends, colleagues, and all the people I met through the years who have given me happiness and fulfillment in my life.

My wife, Judy, assisted me with this project every day for two years, helping me with my recollections and refining my ideas. Her insight, encouragement, and particularly her patience were immeasureable.

I would like to thank my daughter, Emily, and Charles Willey of PC Professor in Florida for their many hours of help with computer technology that I so desperately needed.

My thanks also to Susan Hayes, my production manager, not only for her enthusiasm, but for teaching me the difference between hyphens, dashes, colons, and semicolons.

Lastly, a very special word about a dear friend of mine, Steven Vincent, who in August 2005, was murdered in Iraq doing what he loved and did so well—investigative reporting. I'm deeply grateful to him for giving me so much of his valuable time. He helped fashion my manuscript by enchancing and guiding me with his brilliant editorial advice.

Steven, rest in peace.

Introduction

Meeting Jackie

It was a sunny March morning in 1963, a day when the big news in the papers was about some new rock and roll band called the Beatles. I was chatting with a client in our shop when a fellow with a Marine buzz-cut and a no-nonsense expression walked in and planted himself just inside the door. Right away, I knew he wasn't there for the antiques. For one thing, he just didn't have the air of an interior decorator—for another, he scanned the room as if casing the place for a stick-up. I didn't see a gun, but if I'd noticed a bulge in the breast of his button-down suit, I would not have been surprised.

Five seconds later, she stepped in behind him. The most famous woman in the world. The First Lady of the United States of America. Jacqueline Bouvier Kennedy.

I felt the air rush from my lungs. Not that I wasn't used to seeing celebrities. My father had founded Newel Art Galleries in 1939 to rent furniture and accessories to Broadway producers for use in theater productions. Because of that, by age thirty-three, I'd seen a parade of stars come through our door. There'd been Greta Garbo, producer Mike Todd, burlesque queen Gypsy Rose Lee, Marlene Dietrich, and Katharine Hepburn.

But this was different. This was *Mrs. Kennedy*. JFK's wife. The last person I'd ever expected to walk into our shop on Second Avenue.

Meanwhile, the client I'd been talking to—a well-known scenic designer for a TV network—was having kittens. "Bruce, Bruce!" he panted. "Oh my God, look who's there!"

I glanced toward the rear of the store where my father was standing, overseeing the whole scene. I gave him a questioning look and he replied with a curt nod—his way of letting me know that I had his confidence in handling the First Lady alone.

"May I help you, Mrs. Kennedy?" There was no point in pretending I didn't know who she was.

"I'd like to look around, if you don't mind," she replied in her soft, wistful voice. She was wearing a powder blue dress with a smart blue beret-like hat. I remember thinking how elegant she looked, how much taller she was in real life than she appeared on TV. "I saw some of your things in Mr. Kenneth's salon, and he mentioned that you might have other items I would find interesting."

Mr. Kenneth was the New York hairdresser responsible for Jackie's celebrated coiffure. A few years back, Newel had sold him a pair of English Regency pier tables adorned with palm motifs. Really nice pieces. Apparently, Jackie had seen them and agreed.

I escorted her around the shop, followed close behind by the Secret Service agent. (His name was Clint Hill, and eight months later he would achieve sad notoriety as the agent who leaped on the back of the presidential limousine to protect Mrs. Kennedy on that terrible day in Dallas.) Jackie explained that she and her husband were building a weekend get-away in the horse country near Middleburg, Virginia. Friends were helping her select furnishings for the home—famous friends like interior decorator Billy Baldwin and Jayne Wrightsman, then a leading figure on the Fine Arts Committee of the White House.

"But I like to hunt for antiques myself," she added.

As I said, we saw many celebrities come into Newel—and after I eventually took over the business, we saw many more. But most of the time they came to our shop to examine props for theater, movie or television productions, or else accompanied by interior decorators who did most of the antiquing themselves. Jackie, however, was on her own—looking, as she told me, for English Regency lacquered furniture, a style dating back to the early nineteenth century.

However, I knew that she had something of a negative reputation among many antique shops in New York. Dealers I had spoken with speculated that the problem was Jack. Back in the late 1950s, when he was a senator, he evidently kept his wife on a skimpy domestic budget. As a result, she frequently had to return many of those items she had taken to try, saying they were too expensive. Incredible as it may seem now, some of my colleagues didn't want to deal with her.

But I didn't care. I wanted to help the First Lady find whatever she was searching for. It was in my blood, my instincts as a decorative arts dealer. Since my childhood, my father had instilled in me a simple lesson. *If you want something in life, don't come back until you find it.*

Back in 1963, Newel hadn't yet become the largest antiques shop in the nation, but we had grown to the point that our Second Avenue shop was dedicated solely to vases, lamps, andirons, and other accessories. Major pieces of furniture were stored in two midtown lofts situated just a few blocks away. I worried that Jackie might not have the time or patience to go through our entire inventory, but when I suggested we visit those two facilities, she nodded vigorously. "Oh, let's go!" I was relieved. The First Lady seemed to be having fun.

Was I nervous? Not as much as you might think. True, this wasn't some millionaire's trophy wife with a bottomless checkbook that I was dealing with here. But as we climbed into the back of the Secret Service car, something else my father taught me came to mind. Don't try to impress people, just be yourself, he often said. And remember—no matter how famous or powerful your clients may be, they come to you as they would a doctor or a lawyer, in need of your expertise and perhaps a little intimidated by *you*. Advice that proved its weight in repoussé Baroque gold plate throughout my entire career, especially when I dealt with famous clients such as Barbra Streisand, Jane Fonda, Yoko Ono, and many others.

Jackie couldn't have been more charming and gracious. Before we set off, she asked Agent Hill to fetch a couple of containers of take-out coffee for us to drink in the car. Then, as we drove through Manhattan traffic, she asked me some questions about myself. How old was I when I started working with antiques? Fifteen, I answered. How did I get started? By following in my father's footsteps, I replied, leaving out the fact that when I was a kid I was more interested in girls and basketball than antiques, but my father wanted me in the business—and in those days, kids were expected to do what their fathers wanted.

She then remarked on my tie, a colorful thing I unfortunately lost over the years. "You make a real fashion statement," she teased.

"Mrs. Kennedy," I said, certain I was blushing, "if tomorrow you should decide to wear boxing gloves, women across America would immediately rush out to buy them." She laughed and I felt pretty darn good.

We spent about two and a half hours together, poking through the objects that were stacked up in the two lofts. Jackie plunged right in, moving aside chairs and tables and cabinets herself to get a better look at what we offered. She expressed astonishment at the range of our inventory, which I explained derived from our theater business. Where else could a time-pressed designer or production stylist find under one roof everything from Renaissance armchairs to twentieth-century commodes?

At the same time, I was impressed by the First Lady's eye. Even amidst all the objects assembled at our two lofts, she spotted just what she wanted. From our Thirty-seventh Street space, she selected a pair of Victorian English papier-mâché chairs, priced at $330 each (in 1996, when Sotheby's auctioned off her estate, one of these same chairs went for $17,250) and a three-piece nineteenth-century red lacquered chinoiserie salon set. From our

Forty-seventh Street facility, she picked out a black-lacquered English Regency chest and stand.

This *really* caught my attention, for so few people in those days had the boldness to mix colors and styles like that. But Jackie could visualize unusual combinations, and she had a strong sense of design. She would have made one hell of an interior designer.

And this, in turn, is why her visit to Newel that afternoon was more than just another visit by a celebrity, albeit one of spectacular fame. For in a sense, it marked the real beginning of my success in the decorative arts, and the wonderful career I subsequently enjoyed in this field. Before Jackie, the rich and affluent *bought* taste because few of them had taste of their own. To America's plutocrats and moguls, taste was European, and Europe meant glitzy French *meubles* tricked-out in more ormolu than a house of ill repute. Or if they wanted the "baronial" look, it was bland English "brown" furniture, whose tepid lines and mahogany woods are the best cure for insomnia I know. No Biedermeier, forget Italian Directoire; Art Deco could have been Regency Martian for all they knew.

Then came Jackie. And once America's "unofficial minister of culture," as she was called at the time, imported a sense of style to the Presidency—and began restoring the White House in 1961 (who can forget her charmingly shy television tour of the residence?)—people woke to the possibilities of a more individual look to interiors. She put interior decorators on the social map, making them as *de rigueur* to the upper-crust lifestyle as a personal banker, a psychotherapist, and a creative accountant. And Newel, with its eclectic inventory, benefited greatly from what

Jackie helped wrought. Later, when I took over the business, I had the fortunate opportunity to confirm and extend America's interest in the outré, rediscovering such styles as Swedish Biedermeier, Art Nouveau, and French '40s, while discovering and naming an entirely new field—so-called "Fantasy Furniture." Even my unearthing of the entire set of panels from the Grand Salon of the ocean liner *Normandie*—one of the greatest Art Deco finds—I can attribute in some way to Mrs. Kennedy's influence in popularizing interest in design, craftsmanship, and fine antiques.

After selecting a few more pieces of furniture, Jackie asked to return to Second Avenue to look over some accessories. There, among additional items, she chose a pair of French Empire-style porcelain urns and two English Bristol-style lamps—bringing her overall total to thirteen objects. (I remember her choices clearly because later she sent a handwritten letter to me confirming her purchases—a letter of course I saved, and still possess, along with other correspondence she subsequently sent to me.)

As we were wrapping up the transaction, it seemed Jackie had something additional in mind. "As you know," she began, "we're finishing up the restoration of the White House. While I was looking through your inventory today, I was keeping an eye out for one last piece we need for a guest bedroom." Opening her purse, she pulled out a photograph of a nineteenth-century American Empire chest of drawers. "If you find something like this, could you send a photo to me? Just write 'private' on the lower left corner of the back of the envelope and the letter will come directly to me."

I took the picture. It was not a particularly fetching piece, I thought — stolid, clunky, made of carved mahogany. But Jackie wanted it and I wasn't about to offer my evaluation. "I'll do my best to find it, Mrs. Kennedy."

We shook hands, then, with a nod to Agent Hill, the President's wife turned and left the shop.

Well! Seems I had a mission. And besides, now my father's stern injunction really took on meaning. *If you want something in life, don't come back until you find it.*

I searched high and low for weeks, looking into every antique shop I knew in and around New York. Sending Jackie photograph after photograph. Receiving in return letters from the First Lady or phone calls from her secretary Mary Gallagher. "No." "Nope." "Not this one." "Sorry." I kept trying.

I started to get a little concerned. How many *other* dealers did Jackie have out there, scouring the territory for that last piece to complete the White House restoration? Maybe one of my colleagues and competitors would come through for her before I could.

"Don't worry," my father told me. "Keep looking and eventually you'll find it." I hoped he was right.

Then, by chance one day, I was walking in the West Forties of Manhattan, when I passed one of the nondescript thrift shops that used to dot the area. And there in the window stood a nineteenth-century American Empire chest of drawers. Quite similar—no, damn near exact—to Jackie's photograph, right down to the wooden drawer pulls.

I immediately ran home, grabbed a camera, rushed back to the shop, and snapped a picture and sent it to Washington. Within days I received a letter from the White House reading, "Mrs.

Kennedy and the Fine Arts Committee have decided to purchase your Empire bureau for the White House collection." Jackie wanted it! I hurried back to the thrift shop and purchased the chest for $90. A few days later, White House Registrar James Ketcham (who later became the official White House curator) arranged for the bureau's delivery to the First Lady. I had done it. I had added my little bit to White House history. Mission accomplished!

I dealt with Jackie several more times after that. In December 1964, when she was moving from Washington to New York, she wrote to me asking if I'd be interested in purchasing a pair of English early nineteenth-century black-lacquered chairs from her own collection. Knowing her taste level, I bought them sight unseen. Today, they decorate the living room of the Manhattan apartment I share with my wife Judy.

In the 1970s, Jackie would occasionally drop into Newel. She seemed to feel comfortable at the shop and enjoyed talking with me about antiques and the arts. On one such visit, I mentioned to her something a mutual friend of ours, the legendary stage designer Oliver Smith, had told me—that she had amassed an exquisite collection of Persian miniatures which she kept more or less in seclusion in the bedroom of her Fifth Avenue apartment.

"It's a shame that no one can see your collection," I said to her.

"But I can see them, Bruce," she replied, with a bittersweet smile that seemed to hint at something both lonely and melancholy inside of her. "That's what's really important to me."

It was the last time I saw her.

★ ★ ★

But that's not the end of the story.

It was another sunny March morning, this time in 1997. I was sitting down in my apartment for Sunday breakfast with my wife Judy, when I happened to glance at the front page of the *New York Times*. There I saw an article by reporter James Bennet poking fun at the then-fresh brouhaha over the Clintons' renting of the Lincoln bedroom to guests who would often pay $10,000 for the privilege of sleeping in the fabled chamber. A friend of mine had done it, and he claimed it was rather awe-inspiring—especially with a vintage copy of the Gettysburg Address hanging on the wall. Another visitor to the bedroom had evidently also been impressed, at least according to the *Times*: ex-governor of Colorado Richard Lamm. In fact, Bennet quoted Lamm in his article as saying, "I'm putting my sweaty running clothes away, and all of a sudden it dawns on me that this was Abraham Lincoln's chest."

It was? I wondered. The following Monday, I called the White House, identified who I was, and after navigating through various receptionists and departments, finally reached the White House curator's office. I identified myself once again, and—without discussing the exact purpose of my call—described the piece of furniture I'd purchased for Jackie, and asked about its current location. A few hours later, the curator's office called me back with an answer to my query. It was what I suspected. The American Empire chest I'd found in a West Side thrift shop in 1963—the boxy, boring mahogany bureau for which I paid $90—was believed to be the actual chest of drawers that honest Abe once used during his administration.

But actually, the whole thing made me feel a little sad. Jackie had asked me to find that chest because she thought it fit a conception she had of the White House. Someone in later years had probably taken the piece from wherever it ended up and stationed it in the Lincoln bedroom because it would provide an "authentic" experience—and additional clothing space—for overnight campaign contributors. In one sense, it seemed like a small betrayal of the sense of style Jackie had tried to bring to the Presidential residence. And in another, it felt like the closing of a circle: at the beginning of my career in the decorative arts, Newel furniture was used as theater props for Broadway plays. Now, near the end, someone was once again using my objects to set a stage, but this time in the very heart of political power.

THE WHITE HOUSE

Dear Mr. Newman —

Our new house wont be ready till the end of April — if by then! but it just has to be.

As I told you it is very hard to visualize it — as it will be an assemblage of things from 4 different houses we have lived in over the past 9 yrs — none of which are together now —

I enjoyed my trips up & down your buildings so much & I would like to ask you if you could do this for me — hold the objets until the end of April when I will send a truck for them (Just a few special ones I am really interested in as I cant ask you to reserve your whole store for me!

, By then I will have the furniture placed - the rooms painted & curtains hung & pictures ready to be hung - so I can tell in a minute if your things will go where in my dreams I see them so perfectly - If any do not work out - may I return them to you within 2 days?

These are the things I would

5) really love you to save — (some of the others
I can tell without trying . them if I want
to order them then)

THE WHITE HOUSE

9065   pr red lacquer side chairs
9063   red lacquer writing table
39013 — terrace lights ('just send 2)
40758   1 Blackamoor low table

3110 2 1 pr black lacquer arm chairs

F 6o124   1 pink gold + black lacquer console

6926   1 Black lacquer chest ~~+ stand~~
                                     ~~+ stand~~

37069 gilt + Black Empire Round back arm chair

          Lamps or urns
1861 1 pr red overlay with black + gold handles —

2)

) the ones I have underlined are the ones I care about most so please put off anyone who wants to come in & snatch them up for just another month —

As you can see I have so much black & gold — They may look marvelous together — or it may be a bit too much — so I really must try them first

Thank you for all your kindness I enjoyed today enormously!

Sincerely

Jacqueline Kennedy

American Empire chest of drawers I found for
Jackie Kennedy when she was renovating the White House.
It now resides in the Lincoln Sitting Room.

(Photo by Bruce White © White House Historical Association)

Part One

From Ellis Island
to
Newel Art Galleries

Chapter One

The Immigrant Makes It

Nearly every afternoon in the early 1940s, residents of the Upper East Side grew accustomed to seeing an old man clop down Park and Fifth avenues in a horse-drawn open wagon. They'd watch as the rosy-cheeked old man stopped in front of residential addresses between Fifty-seventh and Ninety-sixth streets, and in a thick Yiddish accent, called out to building superintendents, "Any stuff today?"

Supers were glad to see the old man. In the days before Christie's and Sotheby's became household names (and later, *The Antiques Roadshow* and eBay), people hadn't yet realized that all the old furniture and knick-knacks they had lying about their homes was valuable property. As a result, when they redecorated their apartments, they simply tossed the out-of-date objects in the basement, expecting maintenance men to dispose of them.

But this gregarious old guy did much of the supers' work himself—for a few bucks, he'd cart away such discarded items as gilt
Louis XV chairs, bronze doré wall sconces, porcelain lamp bases,
and various accessories nobody wanted any more. What would
these people think now! Then he'd move to the next building
and call out, "any stuff today?" When his wagon was full with a
rich antiques trove, he'd make his way downtown to a shop on
Second Avenue and Forty-seventh Street, the original location of
Newel Art Galleries.

The man's name was Sam Goldberg. He worked for my father. My father, who never went to public school, possessed the
razor-sharp instincts of a born entrepreneur. He founded Newel
in 1939 to supply props to Broadway productions. Never one to
think small, he wanted the biggest, best, most complete holdings
of old, strange, and unique objects in the city, and constantly
sought out untapped sources of material. Sending old Goldberg
to scour the Upper East Side with horse and wagon—something
no other antiques dealer had thought of before—was one way he
improved his inventory, kept the edge on his competitors, and insured that theater producers returned to Newel. As for the objects
themselves, my father didn't seem to care what period they were.
Antiques, he always maintained, were just *product,* a means to feed
his family.

A hard-nosed guy, my father. Yet it was he who provided the
background in which I developed my enthusiasm for the decorative arts—a deep, abiding passion second only to my love for my
wife Judy and daughter Emily. And there is no way I can tell my
story, or convey to you my joy in spending a life among some of

the most beautiful objects on earth, without telling his story. My father towered over me in life, casting a patriarchal shadow in which discipline was often indistinguishable from warmth, and fatherly affection bought by obedience. Yet thirty-three years after his death, the tensions, frustrations, and desperate love I felt for him still haunt me. Not a day goes by that I don't think of him.

But there's another aspect to my father's story that's important to relate. It has to do with history. His life touched many significant moments of the modern age: the immigration wave of the early 1900s, the rise of movies, the Depression, the advent of television, the assimilation of ethnic groups into the American middle class. Combined with my experiences from the 1950s onward, our lives form a 100-year long tale that stretches from Ellis Island to the Upper East Side, and centers around home and family, work and success, Old World values and New World freedom. In its own way, it is *the* classic story of twentieth-century America. And it's main theme, the axis around which many of my family's struggles and passions turned, is the world of antiques and decorative art—the world that links my father's story to mine, and binds us both to the American Dream.

The first thing my father did when he came to the New World was have an accident in his pants. The year was 1902, and little Meyer Newman, dressed in a sharp black velvet suit, was two years old. I mention this unappealing fact because it underlines one of the obstacles my ancestors faced as soon as they reached America—no one spoke English. Not even enough to get my poor besmeared father some help. (His predicament did, however, lead to a long-standing family joke that Meyer "arrived in New York with a load in his pants.")

It must have been quite a scene. My grandparents, together with five daughters, three sons, and all their belongings standing goggle-eyed on the crowded dock of Ellis Island. They'd come from the area around Elizavetgrad, in southern Russia, a town with a population then of some 32,000. They were no doubt thankful to get away. In 1881, Elizavetgrad (now called Kirovograd) had been the epicenter of a bloody pogrom that had killed dozens of Jews and left thousands homeless. Anti-Semitism always lurked just beneath the surface of life back there and, in fact, a second pogrom erupted around the town in 1905. But by then, my family was already three years beyond the Pale, struggling in conditions in America that, while tough, were at least not lethal.

I'm not sure of my family's original name. Like so many immigrants, they may have Anglicized something unpronounceable to Americans. Or some functionary at Ellis Island may have barked something to my grandfather like "all right, you're the 'new man,'" and the moniker stuck. In any case, my family were total *greeners*. Within a few months, they lost, or were swindled out of, most of the money they'd brought with them from Russia. The New World's streets may have been paved with gold, but for the Newman's, their American journey had to begin from scratch.

The family settled on Kosciusko Street in the Williamsburg section of Brooklyn. From what I've gathered, my grandfather—who had been a farmer in Mother Russia—began selling shoes, and perhaps clothing. My father rarely spoke of those days. His father died when he was still a small boy. By age fifteen, my father was selling vegetables out of a horse-drawn wagon. He worked for a while at the Schaefer Pen and Pencil Company. He knocked about in odd jobs to help support his family and never had the chance to go to school. He grew up strong, lean, wiry, a handsome young man with a head of thick jet-black hair. Like most immigrant sons at that time, he did whatever he could to bring money in for the family. I guess I shouldn't wonder why he never waxed nostalgic about the "old days."

But then Fate lent him a hand. A *big* hand, in the form of a new entertainment medium that was then sweeping the nation—motion pictures. When my father was around eighteen, he landed a job at an outfit called Burns & Co. Burns' *raison d'etre* was renting furniture and accessories to movie studios for their sets. Although the movie industry had, by 1920, largely decamped for California, there were still studios cranking out silent films—Paramount had its Astoria Studio in Queens, for example, and Thomas Edison's own production company was hanging on in the Bronx. Fortunately, my father's decision to work at Burns eventually changed his entire life and set the stage for everything to come—including my own career in the antiques field.

He couldn't have known this at the time, of course. Movies for him were just, well—*movies*. Besides Coney Island, they were one of the few ways people in his social and economic class escaped the daily fight for survival. He'd chaperone his younger siblings to the local "theatre," where they'd take in the latest extravaganza starring Rudolph Valentino, Theda Bara, or Douglas Fairbanks, Jr. Then they'd return to their cramped Brooklyn apartment, imaginations afire with images of impossibly glamorous people living romantic lives in the most exotic settings—all for a nickel!

But movies for my father weren't only escapist entertainment. As soon as he began working at Burns, he realized that the silver screen offered golden opportunities for anyone with ambition. And indeed, one day he saw a well-known movie set designer in Burns' showroom, looking around for assistance. Although his job at the time was a mere furniture handler, my father leaped to the designer's side, and had soon rented him a truckload of material. His boss was so impressed by the young man's moxie (There's a great old-fashioned word that fits my father perfectly!), he promoted him to salesman on the spot. The Newmans were thrilled.

But my father did not intend to stop there. Not with his tenacity. If decorative movie props were his meal ticket, then, by God, he was going to become an expert in them. And to do that, he turned to one of history's great democratic institutions, a flower of man's age-old pursuit of learning and enlightenment: the New York Public Library. Traveling to Forty-second Street after work, he began spending evenings in that ornate building reading books and magazines and soaking up knowledge about art, design, antiques, and architecture.

In his own way, my father formed part of a social movement that was beginning to transform America. Like so many other changes to this nation, it started with the movies. With their extravagant sets that conjured spectacles ranging from the fleshpots of ancient Egypt to the imperial courts of Europe and more, movies expanded the public's awareness of what *interior spaces*

looked like—or could look like, given enough money and imagination. For most of history, rooms with expensive furnishings,
artwork and antiques were the purview of kings, nobles and later,
the very wealthy. But with movies, the average person could for
the first time view such opulence—however fanciful or kitschy—
for themselves. Scenes from such visually ravishing films as *Intolerance, Ben-Hur, Cleopatra, The Thief of Baghdad,* and so many others,
gave people a glimpse of how the glamorous and more fortunate
lived years before Robin Leach dreamed up his television pro-
gram, *Lifestyles of the Rich and Famous.* Add in the magnificently
appointed movie theaters themselves, and suddenly, objects that
spoke of history, age, craftsmanship—in short, *antiques*—became
part of the common imagination. In time, they would become
part of the American way of life.

I hear my father say (and I still hear his voice every day) that
antiques were objects to rent, not *objets d'art.* But I wonder. People in 1920 may have marveled at the sets of *The Four Horseman
of the Apocalypse,* or Grauman's richly decorated theaters in L.A.;
still, only the rich, counseled by such advisers as Joseph Duveen
and Bernard Berenson, had any real interest in *owning* art or antiques. But my father's drive to study the decorative arts leads me
to think that, even at an age when antique dealers were rarer than
Democratic presidents, his passion for historical objects went beyond their use as mere props. I think he truly loved old things.
He might not have been able to articulate that love himself,
but in another era, perhaps, if economic survival was not such a
pressing issue, he might have become more of a traditional dealer.

His efforts at self-education did not go unnoticed. Struck by
my father's presence in the reading room every night, a librarian

asked him why he pored so fervently through the piles of books stacked beside him. When he told her about his deepening interest in the fine and decorative arts, she suggested he pursue his studies in college. "I can't," my father confessed. "I have no educational background." Impressed by my father's dedication and commitment, the librarian promised she'd help him out—and, in a wonderful act of kindness, wrote about his situation to the head of admissions at Cooper Union for the Advancement of Science and Art. A few months later, the tuition-free university—founded in 1859 by another self-made entrepreneur with no schooling, Peter Cooper—accepted my father for night classes. He enrolled in 1920, and two years later, received a certificate of achievement in art and architecture.

I picture my father stepping out of Cooper Union, certificate in hand. And I see a young man born in a far-away country where opportunities for the poor—let alone Jews—were almost nonexistent, who, through hustle, work, and luck, was on his way to attaining the American Dream. He wasn't alone, of course: there were thousands, perhaps millions, of young men like him, each prospering from the then-booming American economy and its open and tolerant democracy. It was unprecedented, a social and historical miracle when you think of it, and I stress the point in part because I'm grateful to this nation and what it offered to my parents' generation.

But I have another reason for dwelling on my family roots. Because of my profession, people who meet me frequently expect me to fulfill a certain stereotype of an antiques dealer—you know, upper-crusty, vaguely English, a member of the polo playing East Hampton set. But that's not me (for one thing, I prefer golf.) I'm the son of immigrant stock who were educated in such democratic institutions as public libraries and tuition-free universities, and who rose up to grab their piece of America. I will never forget where my roots came from, nor will I ever forget that, in the end, I'm just a kid from Brooklyn.

It's like my father told me. "Be honest. The only way you get ahead is by being yourself. The truth is always the best lie."

Encouraged by his newly acquired education and the high economic tide of the Jazz Age, my father decided to go it alone. He left Burns, bought a truck and began hauling furniture and props for theatrical companies. Later, he added delivery routes to and from department stores. By 1925, he'd expanded his business into a mini-fleet of six trucks. Then, in 1926, he expanded his life in a different direction. He married his bookkeeper.

Her name was Evelyn Kantor. She was nineteen years old, the Brooklyn-born daughter of a pants manufacturer who had emigrated from Amsterdam in 1904. In 1927, my sister Marilyn was born, followed by Beverly in 1928. Then it was my turn, a bouncing eight-pound baby boy who greeted the world in 1930.

There we were. The next generation of Newmans, the first completely born in the New World. And there I was, a kid with two sisters. Two older sisters who, for all the world, seemed completely normal, loving girls. Only later in life, when my father was preparing me to inherit the business did Marilyn and Beverly reveal themselves as being as envious as they were—a transformation that became particularly grotesque after my father's death when they tried to keep the control of Newel from me. The fight for the company tore our family apart.

But that was in the future. By the early 1930s, my father had his own problems: bankruptcy. At the time of the '29 market crash, his business increasingly involved department store deliveries. These stores usually paid thirty to sixty days after billing, and when money began to dry up as the Depression took hold, the stores simply stopped paying. To keep afloat, he began selling his trucks, letting workers go, until finally, like so many other small and large business owners, he went belly up.

Today, I can't imagine the anxiety my parents suffered wondering how to make ends meet and support three children. On the other hand, *my* recollections of the Depression were of a happy, carefree time. My first memory is chasing a Good Humor truck down the block, hoping to buy a popular ice cream treat that sometimes had the words "Lucky Stick" printed on its wooden handle—find that, and you'd get another ice cream free. Other than that, I remember playing stickball and basketball and going to the movies—all the usual things kids did in those days. My father managed to keep us clothed and fed. His children had no inkling of the hard times faced by his generation. We were sheltered, protected, and loved.

We were also surrounded by antiques. I remember that quite vividly. During his trucking days, my father would purchase a lamp here, a table there, along with various assorted accessories until our apartment bulged with unique and unusual things. One piece in particular caught my imagination: an eccentric-looking lamp that consisted of a two-foot tall bronze serpent, etched with scales, coiling up to a beaded lampshade. In the inexplicable way kids fixate on things, I'd stare at the lamp, examine it, wonder who made the object, what the serpent signified. Was it a demon, a guardian, a monster? I kept that lamp with me during my entire career at Newel, although I never let on what it meant to me. That turned out to be a mistake. About five years ago, I left for lunch one afternoon, only to discover upon my return that my nephew Lewis Baer, who worked at the shop and ultimately purchased the business after my retirement, had sold the piece to a passing designer. I was devastated—for sixty-five years I'd lived with that lamp—but I couldn't blame Lewis, I'd never told anyone how I felt about it.

Fortunately, I was destined to deal with many more antiques than just a single serpent lamp.

Throughout my career, people have constantly asked how Newel was started. Here's how: my father and mother assembled around twenty antique accessories from our house, loaded them in the rumble seat of their Nash sedan and—leaving sandwiches for us kids to eat—took the objects to a small shop they rented on Second Avenue and Forty-seventh Street. There, they laid the antiques on a ten-foot long table stretching in an otherwise empty store and declared Newel open for business. When those objects had been rented out, they replenished the company's stock with additional accessories. Now for me, at age nine, Newel's birth was traumatizing. All I knew was that my parents were taking antiques out of the house and returning later in the evening without them. Were we moving? What were they going to take away next? Soon, of course, I learned the truth and accepted the firm as my father's new business. And over the years, I never allowed myself to forget how Newel began, and where all my good fortune started: with twenty antiques displayed on a ten-foot table in an empty store.

In 1939, with the American economy beginning to improve, my father plunged back into the prop-renting business with Newel Art Galleries. I'm not sure about the genesis of the name—it was probably a combination of "New" for Newman and "El" for Ellis, for Ellis Marks, an old buddy from the Burns days whom my father hired to work at his new business. (Marks, however, had no financial interest in the firm.) As for "Art Galleries"—although the firm was not a gallery, and didn't sell "art," I imagine my father simply wanted to give his company some class to set it apart from his competitors. He never wanted Newel to be just any antiques shop, and it never was.

Using his past experience in the business, my father developed what we'd call today a smart "business plan." He approached Broadway set designers (movie studios, of course, had by now all moved to Hollywood) and asked them to provide design sketches for their upcoming shows. Then he went to antiques dealers around the city and took various objects on consignment. Designers went through the cache and selected the items they wanted for their sets. My father rented each object for ten weeks, on an installment plan basis, charging ten percent of the object's list price each week until the item was paid for. But he asked for three weeks rental in advance, and with that money would purchase each selected object from whatever dealer he'd originally obtained it. In this way, he maintained a steady flow of money and inventory.

If you look back in old *Playbills* from the 1940s to the 1980s, you'll find Newel credited with furnishing the props for countless Broadway plays: a partial list of original productions includes *Angel Street* (1941), *The King & I* (1951), *Tea and Sympathy* (1953), *The Sound of Music* (1959) and *La Cage aux Folles* (1983). The list of revivals for which Newel provided props literally runs into the hundreds.

As a kid I'd sometimes hang around Newel after school, running errands and carrying out odd jobs. Even then I noticed what a tight ship my father ran. He never sat down in front of his employees, never let them see him reading the newspaper or doing anything that was not work related. He was friendly, open and fair with his employees, but he never, for a moment, relinquished his air of probity, honor, and dedication. Part of his attitude was the way men of that time were expected to act, of course; part, no doubt, stemmed from the rigors of his background. But most of his integrity, I believe, came from some source deep within him, which I always, from childhood onward, acknowledged with fear, respect, and awe.

When I was around twelve, an event occurred that had enormous impact on my life. On the surface, it was a small thing: my father asked me to purchase some three-penny nails. I drifted down to the local hardware store, asked the man for some nails, and when told there were none in stock, returned to my father empty-handed. I'll never forget the look he gave me. It was worse than a beating, an Old Testament scowl expressing surprise, disappointment, and wrath. "Why are you just standing there? Go to another store—and another and another if you have to!" he commanded. "When you want something in life, son, *don't come back until you find it.*"

You can bet I scoured every store in the neighborhood— and beyond — for three-penny nails. I found them, too. And just like heeding my father's injunction, years later, I unearthed and obtained the thousands of treasures I set my sights on. But that's what a father's example can do for a son: set a standard of behavior that you'd rather die for than fail to meet.

I mentioned my father's integrity a moment ago. I want to tell you one more story to underline my point. The story's incomplete—but for reasons you'll soon understand. One day, Goldberg returned from one of his Upper East Side missions with a large, ornate secretary lashed to his wagon. I happened to be at the shop that afternoon and watched my father inspect his new acquisition. Lo and behold, what should he discover in a drawer but a secret compartment, inside of which lay a small book—a handwritten diary, actually. Skimming the pages, my father let out a slow whistle. Then he sat down, and reread the diary, more slowly this time. When he finished, he stood and, without a word, placed the pages in a cast-iron stove and burned them. Within moments, the entire diary was destroyed.

Years later, I asked my father what the pages had revealed. He told me that in the nineteenth century the secretary had evidently belonged to one of the most prominent American families, whose name he then disclosed. The man's wife had written the diary and hid it inside the desk, where, for unknown reasons, it had been lost and forgotten. In those pages, however, the man's wife confessed that she was in fact Jewish, her father was a tailor—and that furthermore, in her younger years she had once been a prostitute. The information would have ruined the woman's historical reputation, and severely embarrassed her descendants. For that reason, my father told me, he had to destroy the diary—even though he could have sold it for a tidy sum. Admiring his decision, I agreed. It was a loss for history, perhaps, but a gain in the general quotient of human kindness.

The woman's name? I'll never tell. Since my father had the integrity to take her secret to his grave, surely you have to expect me to do the same.

Chapter Two

The Brighton Pavilion
Seals the Deal

I didn't watch TV game shows much, but I knew who she was: Dorothy Kilgallen, the shrill-voiced panelist on the famous quiz show *What's My Line?* One afternoon in the mid-1950s, she and her husband, Broadway actor and producer Richard Kollmar, visited Newel. I remember everyone's excitement as Ellis escorted the couple through the shop. Even our bookkeeper, Miss K. a middle-aged woman who generally kept to herself, stepped from the back of the store to take a look.

I guess everyone considered *What's My Line?* special, because by then, famous people had become pretty common at Newel. *Very* famous people in some cases: as I mentioned earlier, every couple of months Greta Garbo would ring our bell. She lived in the neighborhood and often spent an afternoon browsing through our inventory (she never bought anything, though.) Once, Katharine Hepburn dropped by. She was dressed so shabbily—hiding from fans, I suppose—that at first I thought she was a bag lady and refused to let her in. There had also been a constant stream of celebrities from New York-based TV shows that rented antiques from us—*Playhouse 90, Your Show of Shows, Philco Television Playhouse,* and others. Years later, we supplied props to *Saturday Night Live,* in addition to several soap operas: if you've ever wondered where the good people of Pine Valley in *All My Children* found such tasteful furnishings, now you know.

But Kilgallen and Kollmar were here to *personally select some antiques,* they informed us. They were remodeling their apartment, and had heard so much about Newel's inventory, they just *had* to visit us to find the *perfect* objects. As public figures known for urbanity and wit, the Kollmars implied, people expected them to possess objects of the utmost taste and quality, with a dash of Bohemian flair. Where else could they go but Newel?

Courteous as always, Ellis helped Dorothy and Dick (as they insisted we call them) select a truckload worth of antiques and accessories—everything from coffee table bric-a-brac to a pair of huge porcelain figures more suited for a Renaissance palazzo than a Manhattan apartment. Off the couple then went, thanking us for helping them decorate. Job well done, we thought—except for Miss K. She seemed uneasy. This surprised us. She was a quiet presence at Newel, rarely venturing an opinion. This time, however, she sensed something strange about the Kollmars—something we clearly missed.

Miss K. was right. Within a few days, Dorothy and Dick returned every object they had taken from Newel. Sorry, no longer interested, they told us, offering no further explanation. We were stumped. What had gone wrong? A few months later we got our answer: a multi-page photo-spread in *Life* magazine featuring Kilgallen and Kollmar "relaxing at home." How glamorous they seemed! How wonderful their apartment looked! Clearly, the pair had *exquisite* taste. And why not? Nearly every object photographed in the magazine had been borrowed from Newel just a few months before. The shop had supplied the couple with an extra veneer of sophistication that dazzled millions of people. Did we get credit? No!

I was terribly disappointed. Although I was in my mid-twenties at the time, this was my first real experience with celebrity narcissism, and I couldn't believe they acted so falsely. Was I naïve? Of course! But this was before celebrity "tell-all" books and the cynical attitude toward the rich and famous that now pervades our culture. In my innocence back then, I tended to see glamorous people as average folks once you got to know them. At least that had been my experience with the first celebrities I met— baseball players.

When I was around sixteen, I landed a job as a turnstile boy at Ebbets Field, home of the Brooklyn Dodgers. I was paid fifty cents a day and allowed to see the game after the second inning. To this day, I can still smell the beer and hot dogs, and hear the roaring crowds—especially in the bleachers, where "Howlin'" Hilda Chester would cheer on Da Bums with her famous cow bell. I met all the Dodger players of those years: Dixie Walker, Mickey Owen, Cookie Lavagetto, and others. They were polite, regular guys. They made me think there wasn't much difference between baseball stars and people like me, one of their fans.

Then there was Marlene Dietrich. In the early 1950s, she came into our shop on the recommendation of her son-in-law, the art director William Riva. She cut her leg on a spiky iron Venetian lantern I'd mistakenly left on the floor. The cut wasn't deep, but the whole world knew that Dietrich had her legs insured for $1 million. My father and I thought we were facing a horrendous lawsuit, but the movie star just asked for a Band-Aid and slapped it on the wound herself. "I baby-sit for my little granddaughter all the time," she said to us with a charming laugh. "I'm forever banging my legs on *something.*" You can't get much more down to earth than that.

So maybe I'd expected more from celebrities. But, in truth, my reaction to Kilgallen and Kollmar went beyond disenchantment with their phoniness. I felt *indignant.* They had used Newel antiques as *props.* In this sense, of course, they had utilized our company exactly as my father intended—to create illusions, stage-sets. But as much as I loved and respected my father, by my twenties, I no longer accepted his view of decorative arts. To me, they were not impersonal things. No, they were highly *personal* objects that possessed their own style, personality—even soul. To treat them as mere instruments struck me as spiritually hollow and arid. But the issue went deeper than antiques. Like many first-generation young men of immigrant parents, I'd begun to yearn for a broader, more emotionally rich world than my Old World father could provide, and increasingly found myself in a struggle to realize it. I was fighting a covert war to become my own person. And, like in so many other aspects of my life, the battleground of this war was family, antiques—and most of all, Newel itself.

Beginning in my mid-teens, my father had me doing various sweeping and fetchit jobs around the shop. I soon graduated to more important tasks such as stripping, bleaching, and waxing pieces of furniture. Although I wanted to be out playing stickball and basketball, I didn't dare refuse. I couldn't even *imagine* disobeying my father, or rebelling against his authority.

As if my father's presence wasn't enough, there was Miss K. Miss K rarely left the shop—or my father's side, for that matter. That's because Miss K. was my mother, Evelyn Kantor. For reasons best known to themselves, my parents never revealed the true identity of the woman who kept the company books—at the shop, my father always referred to her as "Miss K." For me, however, the problem was the fact that my mother and father were both working at Newel so I was under constant parental surveillance. I hardly had a moment to myself. Concepts like "the generation gap," "do your own thing," "question authority"— ideas which became so familiar in the 1960s were unthinkable to me then.

But fate has a way of unexpectedly planting seeds that can, with time and patience, grow into a sense of purpose and self. When I was in my late teens, for instance, I lived across the street from the Brooklyn Museum of Art, where I spent many an afternoon wandering its cavernous halls. And though innumerable objects and exhibitions surrounded me, I always found myself standing entranced before some large-size statues in the museum's Egyptian wing. Something about the scale of the ancient statues, their appearance and origin, fired my imagination. Without realizing it at the time, I was beginning to appreciate the *essence* of objects, and to hear the mysterious music that emanates from their material, design, and history. I was, in short, falling in love with antiques.

I was also falling in love with the Brooklyn Museum of Art. For much of my life, the BMA served as a source of education, stimulation, and pleasure. Years later, after I'd become successful running Newel, I returned my thanks to the institution by giving it numerous pieces of decorative arts, including a late nineteenth-century day bed by the outstanding American furniture designer George Hunzinger. In 1989, the then BMA director Robert Buck saw the exhibition "Fantasy Furniture" I curated at New York's National Academy of Design. Saying how much he loved the spectacular show, and knowing what a committed supporter I was of his museum, he asked if I might donate to the BMA a piece or two from my personal collection. Our discussions soon grew into the development of an entire museum gallery, containing fourteen pieces of Fantasy Furniture—including an early twentieth-century Black Forest carved bear bench, a late nineteenth-century Venetian Grotto pair of chairs, and a late nineteenth-century antler smoking stand. Called the Judith and Bruce Newman Gallery, it opened with great fanfare in September 1992, and for years remained one of the museum's most popular attractions.

But like all-too-many love affairs, mine with the BMA ended in betrayal and hurt feelings. In 1998, Arnold Lehman, the new director of the museum, asked if I'd agree to let the furniture in the Newman Gallery leave on a world tour—"maybe even Japan would be interested!" he enthused. "Of course," I told him.

Lehman then had the pieces put in "temporary" storage down in the BMA's basement, and filled the now *ex*-Newman Gallery with the "Matthew Scott Sloan" collection of American furniture. Today, fourteen pieces of Fantasy Furniture still languish in the basement. The show never materialized—and in fact, although Lehman had promised to keep me informed about the responses from various museums to the offer of the exhibit, I never heard from him again about it. It appears to me that his enthusiasm about a "worldwide tour of Fantasy Furniture" may have been a ploy to clear out space in the museum for the Sloan collection. Of course, Judy and I never assumed that Fantasy Furniture would be a permanent exhibition, but we did expect that when the BMA eventually ended it, they'd do so with proper appreciation and respect, which Lehman never did. But if you walk through the museum today you'll find none of our Fantasy Furniture pieces on display. Not one. You would have assumed that Lehman would have exhibited at least one with an explanation that the piece was part of a larger collection that the BMA hopes to display again in the future. There is, however, a postcard in the museum gift shop of the Black Forest bear bench—but the card does not acknowledge that the bench came from the collection of "Judith and Bruce Newman." So I ask you: if this is how Lehman treats museum benefactors, does this make you want to donate to the Brooklyn Museum of Art?

But, I digress. As I moved through my teens, my budding appreciation of the beauty of the decorative arts was in constant danger of smothering beneath the weight of my father's all-business attitude. Fortunately, help was close at hand: Ellis Marks. About five years younger than my father, Ellis was an affable

fellow with a dry, self-effacing wit and a face that somewhat resembled Clark Gable's. He loved antiques, especially the way they
were made; he was a crackerjack restorer, repairer, fix-it man—a
veritable jack-of-all-trades. I followed him around Newel, fasci-
nated by his know-how, eager to absorb what I could. By the
time I was seventeen, he'd imparted to me a working knowledge
of woods, marbles, metals, paints, lacquers, hinges, screws, bolts—
in short, the *thing-ness* of antiques.

In many ways, my father and Ellis couldn't have been more
different. My father had a keen eye for objects that could be
rented; Ellis saw how they were *made*. My father was not social,
preferring to spend leisure hours swapping anecdotes about the
antiques trade with business cronies; Ellis loved customers and
was a great salesman, particularly with set designers, to whom he
frequently gave suggestions and advice on how best to use Newel
antiques. Where my father was content to rent objects until they
became too worn for use, Ellis thrived on restoring antiques and
bringing them back to life. But most of all, where my father was
a stern, unyielding patriarch, Ellis was a warm, easy-going com-
panion, unafraid to relate to me on a personal level.

If a man is lucky, he finds a person in his life who opens
doors, expands psychological and emotional dimensions, helps
transform him into the adult he is destined to become. Ellis was
that person for me. I owe him more than I can ever calculate. Indeed, if Ellis Island was my father's gateway to a new world, Ellis
Marks was mine. Years later, he worked for me at Newel, until he
passed away in 1987. But even at the end of his life, I never
stopped seeing him as my mentor. More than a mentor, actually,
more even than an uncle-figure, Ellis was to me a second

father—and a secret ally in my struggle to free myself from all outside influences.

At eighteen, the combination of paternal pressure, Ellis' presence, and my own inner drives, led me to consider a career in the decorative arts. Of course, my father—being my father—had already decided that I was going to follow him in business, and what's more, that I would pursue a formal education in architecture and design. I did have one say in the matter, though: rather than Cooper Union, I enrolled at Pratt Institute. Not only was Pratt one of the leading art and design institutions in the nation, it was located in my beloved Brooklyn. What's more, it had a basketball team that regularly played some of the best college teams in the country.

Antiques and basketball: those were the twin poles around which I centered much of my collegiate activity. As a scrappy, play-making forward on Pratt's basketball team, I had great fun. I loved the flow of the game, its teamwork and sense of "poetry in motion." Even today, I still look back fondly on Pratt's contest against St. John's University in 1951—the year St. John's won the national championship—when I scored points off the late, great, future Hall of Fame coach, Al McGuire. We lost, however, by more points than I care to admit.

As for antiques, well, that became something of an ideological issue. In every project I designed at Pratt, I made sure to include an antique. My idea for a tasteful business office contained a Biedermeier secretary; my library design was adorned with a bamboo *étagère*. My teachers hated it. These were the days of high Modernism in design and architecture: Le Corbusier, *Domus* magazine, super-sleek cabinetry by Charles and Ray Eames, objects made of plastic, fiberglass, and latex. Everything clean, modern, and angular. And marching in lockstep, my teachers at Pratt wanted only the *au courant*, the contemporary. To them, a sinuous little Art Nouveau table lamp was like the mouse in "Dumbo," whose mere appearance sends the huge, lumbering elephants fleeing in terror.

Especially the head of the school's interior design department, Miss Eleanor Pepper. She, too, was a member of the Church of Soulless Modernism. My focus on antiques seemed to get under her skin like a cherry-wood splinter. Adding to her opinion of me as an irreverent yahoo, basketball practice forced me to miss numerous classes during winter semesters. Before long, I sensed she had it in for me.

Matters between us reached a head during my final year at Pratt. One afternoon, as part of my senior thesis, I was giving a lecture on the place of antiques in the history of interior design. The room was packed—my passion for antiques had rubbed off on the students and faculty at Pratt and dozens of people had come to hear me. Speaking—as I normally do—without notes, I'd just begun discussing the great eighteenth-century French porcelain factory, Sèvres, when in walked Miss Pepper. Rattled, perhaps, by her presence, I accidentally inverted two consonants and pronounced the factory "Serves." Someone giggled. Knowing I had screwed up, I nevertheless continued my error, acting as if I'd done it on purpose. If nothing else, I could see I was driving Miss Pepper crazy.

"Mr. Newman," she interrupted, unable to take it any longer. "I believe the fine antique dealers on *Madison Avenue* pronounce the word 'Sev-ruh.'"

"Miss Pepper," I retorted, suppressing a smirk, "I believe second-hand dealers on *Second Avenue* pronounce it 'Serve.'" Everybody burst out in laughter. Miss Pepper's face turned redder than a Japanese cinnabar lacquer box. I don't remember the grade I got in her class, and it's probably just as well.

As we get older, and we reflect on the critical points of our lives, it often seems clear how events form inevitable patterns: of course, you think, my life couldn't have turned out any other way. We often forget that at the time we were actually living these moments, we experienced mainly doubt and confusion and had no idea where the hell we were going. Especially when we were young, and *everything* seems full of doubt and confusion.

I was no exception. By my twentieth year, I could feel a strong momentum in life pushing me toward the decorative arts, and felt little urge to resist it.

It was my father who, without knowing it, showed me the way. When I was about twenty-one years old, he took me to Europe to teach me the tricks of purchasing antiques and decorative objects from Parisian dealers. On our way to the Continent, we stopped off in England, and traveled to a town thirty-seven miles south of London. There, in a ramshackle seaside resort, my father introduced me to an astonishing sight: the Royal Pavilion at Brighton.

Actually, "astonishing" does not do justice to the Brighton Pavilion. Built over a thirty-five-year period beginning in 1787, it is one of the most exotic, over-the-top, jaw-dropping buildings in the world. The exterior of the multi-winged structure is an eccentric amalgam of Classical, Indian, and Chinese motifs, excessive in every detail. The interior is enriched with crystal chandeliers, cast-iron palm trees, domed ceilings adorned with gilded scallop shells, hand-knotted carpets, Chinese wallpaper, dragons, serpents, leopards—a bizarre, and yet thoroughly English expression of Empire, narcissism, magnificence and whimsy. Picture a combination of San Simeon and Xanadu, glimpsed through the opiate dreams of a royal dandy. The Prince of Wales, who later would be King George IV, a rakish mama's boy called "Prinny" by his friends, and the guiding light behind this Regency fun house.

Now, Newel had some unusual pieces, but *nothing* like this. I couldn't believe my eyes. I felt as if I was standing in the land of Oz; the outside world had fallen away, replaced by a phantasmagoria of rich lacquered color, silk embroidery, elephants, houri statues—it was a daydream, it wasn't reality. It tickled my emotions, while its playfulness appealed to my craving for movement, color, freedom. And it was at that moment that I *knew*, without a doubt, that I loved the decorative arts—and more specifically, I loved exotic and unique objects. It was as if the Brighton Pavilion was Newel expanded onto a larger, more elaborate canvas. But there was one difference: amidst these "Hindoo-Gothic" walls, my father's hard-nosed business attitude and constricted emotion did not hold sway. Here, instead of a grim struggle for survival was a sense of happiness, innocence, and *joie de vivre*.

The Pavilion swept me back to the world of the Prince Regent—a man who clearly possessed a deep love of sensuality and make-believe, who seemed to enjoy life. Of course, Prinny was a libertine and a womanizer, an alcoholic and laudanum addict, whose inveterate gambling threw him into debt and made him the despair of his father. He died at sixty-eight, having served ten years as king—but he lived enough for three lives. He was the rebellious, devil-may-care prodigal son I'd secretly wanted to be. In the lush caverns of his palace, he was invisible to the supervising eyes of his parents. He was free — free to be himself.

And that's when I came to a life-changing realization. Yes, I would become an antiques dealer. Yes, I would particularly focus on the most imaginative and playful furniture I could find. But more importantly, I understood, as if the Prince Regent were himself whispering in my ear, I could go into the decorative arts field and in the world of fantasy furniture, *I could be my own man.*

Thank you, Prinny.

About a year after I graduated from Pratt, I received a piece of correspondence from my Uncle Sam that many young men also received at that time: a draft notice. In a strange twist of fate, I spent much of my early military service stationed at Fort Dix, New Jersey, only a few miles from New York. Because of my experience in props and stagecraft I managed to wrangle a job designing and hosting small theater productions and reviews for enlisted men. It got me off the base, not to mention the fact that I was one of the few buck privates in the U.S. Army to have a sergeant act as his chauffeur! We'd take a military-issue truck into New York and drop into Newel, where I'd selected various objects for my shows. I have to admit, I loved showing up at the shop in my G.I. khakis and see the expression on my parents' face. "My son, the soldier," my father would say with pride. After only a few months of military service, however, I broke my wrist (the same wrist I'd injured three times earlier playing basketball) in a bus accident at Fort Dix—an "un-united fracture," to be exact, so severe that the government forced me to accept a medical discharge. Alas, all glory is fleeting, the poets say—and Bruce Newman, heroic warrior, became a civilian once again.

I moved into Manhattan and bought a blue Corvette convertible. It was a great time to be in New York. I had an education, a job, a unique vision of the decorative arts, I'd completed my military duty and the Cold War years were flush. And best of all, I was right in the thick of the 1950s Greenwich Village scene—you know, jazz, coffee shops, bongos, Beatniks, "Ban the Bomb" buttons. (At a small hang-out off Sheridan Square I befriended a young actor who continually hit me up for money, usually to buy gasoline for his motorcycle; years later, he made something of a name for himself: Steve McQueen.)

But as Dwight and Mamie vacated the White House for Jack and Jackie, I began to feel a little dissatisfied. I needed something more. Something to fill an emptiness in my life that even the supple sweep of an Art Deco black lacquered wood and nickel-steel occasional table could not fulfill. I knew there had to be such a thing out there for me—but where?

In the course of time, I found it. In New Hampshire, of all places. Dating from the late 1930s, with tapered legs, a rich blond color and a patina, that to my eyes, lay somewhere between the palest Zinfandel blush and moonlight on a quiet lake. *This* was a real treasure, hardly an antique, of course, but still, a one-in-a-million find. And even better, she looked great in a tennis outfit.

Chapter Three

Family Interference

Her name was Judith Brandus. I met her in 1959 on the sun-splashed tennis court of the Lake Tarleton Club, near Pike, New Hampshire. And although the lake and the White Mountains formed a spectacular backdrop, she was the only thing I saw. I hung out by the court kibitzing while she played, and after her matches, a group of us went for lunch. As charming as I thought I was, Judy hardly gave me the time of day. She did reveal, how-ever, that she worked as an assistant personnel director at the Hertz Corporation and that, surprise, surprise, she came from Brooklyn. Not only from Brooklyn—she and I, it turned out, had been born a block and a half from each other. Two hundred and eighty-five miles from home, and I was smitten with a pharma-cist's daughter from my own neighborhood. There's destiny for you!

Judy also gave me her phone number—a good sign—but being without pen or pencil, I had to commit the digits to memory. Now, numbers have never been my strong suit—I can barely recall the date, let alone a phone number. But for some reason, Judy's stuck in my mind as if it had been embossed there. A few days after returning to the city, I telephoned her. "My friends warned me not to call too soon or I'll look like I'm too interested in you," I said. Not the cleverest way to line up a date, but it worked. She went out with me. Forty-six years later, she's still going out with me.

By the early sixties, as I mentioned, I was living in my own Manhattan apartment, although my parents helped pay my rent and other living expenses. Their way, I suppose, of maintaining control over me. Today, you hear talk about how people remain in adolescence for longer periods of their lives—through their twenties, often into their thirties. You might say I was ahead of my time. At thirty-one, I was a professional antiques dealer, respected by my peers and well educated in many aspects of the trade—but in nearly every other respect, I was still a young man, living in my father's shadow. Why, I was still *single*, for God's sake—a fact that had begun to scandalize my relatives. When is Bruce going to settle down? they wondered. What they didn't know, of course, was that I was deliberately, if unconsciously, holding off making major life decisions until I felt I was my own man, with my own authority.

Newel was the key to it all. My existence, my future, revolved around the shop. Once I gained control of the family business, I thought, I would *finally* be the master of my own fate, and free to move forward with the ideas I'd gained at Brighton and Pratt. I had big plans for Newel: I would concentrate more on retail sales, for example, and advertise in trade and popular publications—in short, I wanted to open the shop up to the public, to make it accessible to as many people as possible. I wanted to *democratize* the antiques field.

In this way, my feelings paralleled, and were reactions to, larger changes taking place throughout the postwar art market. I've already remarked on how the sumptuous interiors depicted in Hollywood movies began to interest Americans in antiques and decorative arts. Then, in 1958, Sotheby's director Peter Wilson—a brilliant, dashing ex-British Intelligence officer said to have been the model for Ian Fleming's James Bond—orchestrated a true art market milestone: the first modern "black tie" evening auction. Promoted by a heavy publicity campaign (including, for the first time, TV coverage), the London-based sale—of seven Impressionist paintings from the Goldschmidt Collection— lasted twenty-one minutes and totaled $1,720,000, the highest amount yet reached at an art auction. More importantly, however, the sale demonstrated that with modern techniques of marketing and hype, auction houses could package high-end art sales as media-friendly "events" which, in turn, could attract a rising class of new collectors. The same people, in fact, that found in Jackie Kennedy—her intelligence, personal style and, in particular, her renovation of the White House—a stimulus for their own interest in interior design. America was on the verge of an explosion in the decorative arts, I felt, and I wanted Newel to be part of it.

But the time was not yet right. Where I wanted to *sell* antiques, my father wanted to *rent* them. He even refused, despite my pleas, to take down the TRADE ONLY sign from Newel's front door.

He saw no reason to indulge the public's new passion for antiques, or to change the business practices that had served him well in the past. And so, the company drifted. Ellis repaired our rental stock, Miss K. kept the books, the occasional celebrity dropped by from television shows or Broadway—like producer Billy Rose, or playwrights Lillian Hellman and George S. Kaufman. Nothing else changed. In the interim, I waited. And waited. Since my father was sixty-four by now, I waited for his eventual retirement.

Meanwhile, Judy and I dated. Ultimately time and maturity weighed in and convinced us both it was time to get married. We announced our nuptial plans in the spring of 1965, expecting joy, relief, and cooperation. Wishful thinking! What we got was quite different.

Contention. Rancor. Everyone had a different idea of what kind of wedding we should have, and where and when we should have it. My parents, Judy's parents, my sisters, even the family dog, I think, offered a suggestion or two. I had no idea weddings entailed so many details, arrangements, complications, decisions! Inevitably, Judy and I took sides—unfortunately, sometimes against one another—and the tension nearly broke us up. There was just so much family pressure on us; we were both still under the domination of our respective parents. Then, at the height of this inter- and intra-family quarreling, my parents left for a sea voyage to Europe. The trip, actually planned months before, would take a month, during which time, it was understood, all combatants in the Bruce and Judy Wedding Fight would cool off and rethink their positions. But rather than easing the situation, Judy and I decided to take the opportunity of my parents' absence to do something audacious, radical, and subversive.

Occasionally I rebelled at the shop in small, unconscious ways. Once, when I was eighteen, my father dispatched me to a auction at Spanierman's Gallery with instructions to purchase lot 141, a large crystal chandelier; instead, I came home with lot 142, a similar object, and he delivered a stinging lecture about my carelessness. Was my error an honest mistake—or a surreptitious mutiny? I couldn't tell you. My mispurchase, however, weighed heavily on my conscience—and I can't tell you how relieved I was when, two years later, I managed to sell lot 142 to an architect designing a hotel lobby.

Then there was the time in my late twenties, when my father allowed me to make an antiques-buying trip to London by myself. His instructions were simple: browse the English shops, spend about $20,000 to $25,000 and ship the material home. But *do not* go to Paris, he commanded, fearing, I guess, that the French dealers would take advantage of me. But after I completed my London business—and made a pilgrimage to the Brighton Pavilion (my third visit by that time)—I just *had* to zip across the Channel to the City of Light. Scouting the Left Bank flea markets one afternoon, I discovered a pair of nineteenth-century carved wooden gargoyles—twisty, humorous, playful pieces, exhibiting the flow and sense of motion I admire in decorative arts objects: the kind of knick-knacks the Prince Regent would have loved, but my father generally ignored. Despite his disciplinary voice in my head, I purchased the pieces. I still have them today, sitting in the entrance hall of my home, where they constantly remind me of my unauthorized journey to Paris.

But this was different. My relationship with Judy was at stake. And if I were ever going to make a stand, now was the time to do it. Even so, to insure that my parents couldn't interfere with our plot, Judy and I waited until they embarked on their week-long return voyage from the continent and we got married. Call it an elopement. In any case, when my mother and father disembarked in Manhattan a few days later, they were met at the pier by a second, younger Mr. and Mrs. Newman. As a new bride, Judy never looked more beautiful.

Her parents were surprised, chagrined, but ultimately relieved by the news. But as I anticipated, mine were disturbed.

For what seemed an eternity, I walked on eggshells around my parents. Remember, during this period, we still all worked at Newel, giving a new definition to "family togetherness." There was no way to escape my parent's silent displeasure. We never talked about the wedding, rarely discussed my fledgling life with Judy, although it was always on our minds. Imagine being with your parents for eight to ten hours each day and unable to talk about your new wife! The tension was unbearable.

Judy and I struggled to make the best of the situation. Stretching our budgets, we got an apartment on First Avenue and Eighty-first Street. At first, she continued working, but at my request, she quit her job. I didn't want her to work. Call me traditional, but I wanted to come home to a wife. Unfortunately, I was only making around $180 a week. I could have earned a larger salary working in another field, but I didn't want to leave Newel. I loved that old shop and dreamed of the day it would be mine. Judy understood and supported my decision. To this day, I marvel at her commitment to the poor, insecure dreamer she married. I guess she really did love me.

And that love showed. We constantly invited my parents

over for dinner, where Judy showered my mother with affection and, most astutely, my father with *respect*. It was slow, tedious work to rehabilitate ourselves in my parents' eyes, but Judy's natural charm and gaiety soon took effect. The first sign of an impending thaw was in 1966, when my father raised my salary to $225, enough to allow us to take a short honeymoon in Puerto Rico. Soon, Judy developed a wonderful relationship with him. His heart melted, and he grew to love her almost as much as I did.

By 1968, the contention that had driven our family apart seemed like a bad dream. In fact, an amazing transformation had taken place. My father, now getting on in years, enjoyed going to Atlantic City, where he'd take long walks down the Boardwalk. Increasingly, he made it clear that he especially enjoyed his walks when accompanied by Judy. My wife's efforts to have a warm relationship with him succeeded beyond our expectations. Indeed, the image of the two of them, arm and arm, strolling past the Boardwalk hotels and amusement park rides of Casino Pier is a memory I'll never forget. Unfortunately, the sight made a deep impression on two other observers, who viewed it with far less satisfaction and pleasure.

My sisters.

Marilyn and Beverly. Beverly and Marilyn. They put me through agony with their acts of hostility toward me. In the early days of my relationship with Judy, everything seemed fine with my siblings. We even asked both of them to be the godparents of our daughter Emily when she was born in 1970. Maybe they secretly thought—or hoped—Judy and I wouldn't last. And maybe I should have seen the signs sooner—my sisters' occasionally odd, standoffish attitude toward my wife, a certain brittleness in their conversations with her.

But if my sisters were somewhat cool in the beginning, once my father began showing favoritism toward Judy—in particular, with those affectionate walks down the Atlantic City board-walk—they turned positively arctic. In front of my eyes, I watched two strong-willed, often bossy but, for all that, generally pleasant women seemed to become manipulative schemers.

There is, at least, something deep and profound about jeal-ous rage—it is a force of nature before which one stands in help-less awe. It's the stuff of sixteenth-century literature, because when I think of my sisters, I think about what those poets wrote about disguised envy. The analogy isn't exact, of course, but only an artist with the psychological insight of Shakespeare could come close to depicting what went on with my siblings. Espe-cially Beverly, the younger daughter, who seemed to harbor the most envy toward Judy: Judy, who was young, pretty and fun. Marilyn had her jealousies, too, but they were more upfront, ra-tional, and ultimately easier to understand—although nonetheless dangerous. And, as it turned out, they both had designs on Newel.

Suppressing all this envy, resentment and need was my fa-ther. Through the strength of his will, he kept the family and Newel together. But as he aged, shadows slowly crept around him. I'm not referring to his health—to the end, he remained a vibrant personality. I'm talking about his loved ones. My mother clung to his authority like it was a rock in a raging sea. I had the impression that Beverly and Marilyn wanted to banish Judy from the family, while disguising their insidious ambitions toward the

family business. Only the love and respect we felt toward him
kept the family from exploding into a million emotional pieces
and destroying everything he spent a lifetime to build.

One late afternoon in April 1972, I was on the roof at
Newel with Alvin Colt, a well-known scenic and costume designer. We were selecting some outdoor furniture and ornaments
for theater sets he was designing, when Ellis came up with the
news that my mother was on the phone, saying it was an emer-
gency. With a sense of foreboding, I rushed down in the elevator,
and took the phone. "Bruce," my mother said in a hysterical
voice. "Come home right away. Your father has collapsed. He's
not breathing."

Chapter Four

The Fight for Newel

I ran from Newel and flagged a taxi to take me to my parents' apartment on the Upper East Side. It was the longest cab ride of my life.

By the time I reached the address, police and paramedics were already on the scene. I burst into the apartment, pushed past some cops and rushed to the side of my mother, seated in the living room in a state of shock. "Are you sure? Are you sure?" I kept repeating, as if unable to believe what had happened.

But at that moment, paramedics came from my parents' bedroom carrying my father's body in a canvas bag. As they passed, my mother let out an anguished sob and I sank slowly on the chair arm beside her. *My God*, I remember thinking, *here is a man whom I loved so much, and who gave me so much, being carted away in a sack. What a way to go.* It was the worst thing I've ever seen in my life.

Freud said that the death of the father is one of the most shattering experiences that can befall a man. It was certainly true in my case. Stunned, speechless, I could only sit beside my mother and attempt to console her even as my own world turned upside down and crumbled into bits.

He had died in his bedroom of a sudden stroke. For the last eight months or so, he'd complained about not feeling well. He went to work at Newel less and less, spending most of his days relaxing with business associates, or taking a stroll through Central Park. His doctor had examined him just a week before and found nothing wrong, so we'd attributed his malaise to the normal condition of a seventy-two-year-old man. His death, then, came as a total surprise—especially to me. I'd always thought my father was larger than life. That he was immortal.

An hour or so later, though, as I was sitting in the suddenly quiet house, a new sensation came over me. Rising through the shock, the pain, the numbness of heart, I felt a growing sense of responsibility. The feeling wasn't exactly conscious, certainly not deliberate, it was as if something outside myself had suddenly granted me permission to act. It was up to me now, I realized. The mantle of family leadership had fallen on my shoulders. For the first time in my life, I had to take charge of a family situation.

There were many things to do. I contacted a funeral parlor, and readied a cemetery plot in the Mt. Carmel Cemetery in Queens. I had to complete these tasks quickly, for although my family was not particularly religious—we generally observed just the High Holy Days—I did want to observe Jewish custom and bury my father within twenty-four hours. I saved one detail for last, however. My father left almost no instructions about how he wished to be buried, but I knew he would not want anything ostentatious. The coffin I selected, therefore, was made of plain mahogany. I realized that it would be hard to take care of this matter, but I had no idea how hard. It is a terrible thing to pick out a coffin for your father.

There was no eulogy; he didn't want one. In fact, it wasn't a big viewing, just family, a few friends, and Ellis. I had requested the funeral parlor to leave the casket closed, for I wanted us to reflect on my father's life, not on his corpse. And while my mother and sisters and even Ellis cried, I remained, for the most part, fairly stoic. I had to be the strong one now. In many ways, I *did* have to be like my father.

At one point in the evening, I found myself alone with him. I put my hand on his coffin, and thanked him for everything he had done for me and given me and taught me and told him I'd take over where he left off—I'd take care of the family and the business; I'd always do what I knew he'd want. But that seemed somehow inadequate. For how do you comprehend a man's life—your father's life—what it meant, the legacy it left behind, the impact it had on your own existence? A man whose life stretched from the old nightmares of persecution and poverty in the Old World to comfort, acceptance, and success in the New, whose personal integrity and ethics inspired deep reservoirs of fear and respect and love from his family—and who bequeathed a profession, a way of life, to me. I could hear his voice in a dozen admonitions, lectures, instructions.

"Be honest, truth is the best lie."

"Two of the most inexpensive tools in life are a smile and a compliment."

"If you come home from work with your hands still clean, you haven't done a full day's work."

"Always wear a suit and tie to work, never let your employees see you sitting around or reading a newspaper—but always treat them and your customers with respect and fairness."

And, of course, what still rings in my mind today: "If you want something in life, son, *don't come back until you find it.*"

Still, there was one thing I'd never hear him say, the one admission I'd waited my entire life for my father to make: that I'd amounted to something, that I'd grown to become a commendable young man—that he was proud of me. Later, when his business friends stopped by the shop to give their condolences, they told me how, during their get-togethers where they would trade anecdotes about the business, he'd talk about me, tell them how wonderful I was, what an asset I was to Newel. He never told me these sentiments, of course, I had to discover his love for me from others. That was just like my father.

One last detail of my father's passing. Months later, I ran into Alvin Colt. I apologized for suddenly running off that day and leaving him alone on Newel's rooftop. He said he completely understood, but, in a good-natured way, let me know that in my headlong rush from the roof, I had forgotten to send the elevator back up to fetch him. Since the elevator was only accessible from the lower floors, Alvin had no way of getting down—and in the shock of events I'd forgotten I left him there. No one heard his knocks or shouts. Hours had gone by, he said, and it was only by the chance visit by an employee that allowed him to escape his enforced isolation and rejoin the world.

★　★　★

My father's death in 1972 precipitated a family crisis that lasted two and a half years and nearly destroyed Newel. All of my future accomplishments—the creation of "Fantasy Furniture," the discovery of the *Normandie* panels, the awards I won and celebrities I met and, perhaps most important, Newel's influence in revitalizing the antiques trade and helping it compete against the auction houses—came within a hairbreadth of never happening.

It went back to the will. My father left my mother everything—including control of Newel. That's what I was *told,* at least, for in reality—and for reasons I've never quite understood—it seemed my mother requested that her lawyer actually keep me from seeing the will. To tell you the truth, at the time, I didn't care much.

The fact that the company was now owned by my mother didn't really trouble me, either. After all, Miss K. had helped found it thirty-three years before and had worked with my father every step of the way. And bequeathing the family business to his wife, I understood, was my father's way of protecting her against financial hardship as she grew older. (If both my parents had simultaneously died, the will, I discovered later, named me sole proprietor of Newel.) What most eased my mind, though, was the realization that my father had painstakingly groomed me to take over the business. My mother, I was sure, accepted this fact and would let me run the shop the way I wanted—in essence, if not by law, Newel was mine. There was one problem, one hitch in my plans that I didn't take into consideration.

Marilyn and Beverly.

In the past, the interest my sisters showed in antiques and the decorative arts could have been placed inside a candlestick snuffer and still have room for the candle. Now, suddenly, with my father gone, they expressed a keen desire to involve themselves with Newel. At the time, I had no clear idea why, only that they began making increasing visits to the shop, to nose around and "learn the business." In time, like certain birds who descend upon and occupy the nests built by other birds, these two came to stay.

They were a complementary pair. Marilyn, the oldest, was an attractive, brown-haired, medium-height woman who had married a good-looking dentist living in Ardmore, Pennsylvania. She had a broad, winning smile, which served, as I later discovered, to hide a calculating mind. Beverly, the more aggressive of the two, was a dark-haired, slim-figured social climber. She married an electrical engineer and moved to his native Montreal, where she bore three children. Although she enjoyed a comfortable life, it seemed to me that she felt compelled to brag about what an important socialite she was in Montreal. And whereas I believed that Marilyn's motives in wanting to control Newel had to do with money, Beverly's, I was convinced, were more devious, involving, at their deepest level, an unadulterated hunger for power.

Although the women maintained jealousies toward one another (Marilyn, in particular, envied Beverly for her supposed social prominence in Montreal), their mutual interests allowed them to work together. One issue in particular joined them together. Neither, I knew, wanted our mother to move in with them. And one way to insure their independence from her, I felt, was to keep her tied to Newel—to make sure, in short, that she never sold the company, or gave it to me.

For nearly three years, my sisters formed a kind of infernal tag-team: first Beverly would "visit" Newel, then, when it was time for her to return to Montreal, Marilyn would take over, leaving only when Beverly came back from Canada. In this way, they slowly began to dominate my mother. Not that they had much trouble: because of her nature, my mother had little willingness to make her own decisions. When pushed, she simply devolved important issues onto a strong masculine figure. To my shock, I realized that figure was not me. It was Beverly, who suddenly revealed a powerful desire to lord over the family as my father once had.

Gradually, though, the situation became intolerable—their condescending attitude and interference with the business was infuriating. This wasn't exactly my idea of discovering the world of freedom and play I'd witnessed at Brighton. To make matters worse, Marilyn's marriage broke up and she stayed for a short time with our mother.

Afraid, I imagined, that Marilyn might have undue influence over her, Beverly came down more often from Montreal. Soon both my sisters were spending entire days at Newel, effectively making it nearly impossible for me to function there. My mother deferred all decisions to her daughters, and especially to Beverly, who now reveled in her role as the family patriarch.

Only now, looking back from a distance of thirty years, do I realize the depths of my sisters' perverse attachment to Newel. Neither of them had much going on in their lives. By seizing control of the company, I believe, they felt, on some unconscious level, that they could, in effect, freeze time. They could keep family matters as they were before my father's death—even, in a weird way, keep him alive by insuring that his legacy never adapted to changing market and social conditions. Even more disturbing was Beverly, who—out of perhaps some desperate in-security or unfulfilled hunger for my father's affection—seemed to want to rule the family and Newel exactly as he had done.

The result for Newel was—nothing. Nothing changed. My suggestions to broaden the scope of the business went nowhere. When I suggested we take down the TRADE ONLY sign and re-move the buzzer from the front door, my mother said no. When I asked for money to advertise in local and trade publications, and when I pleaded with her to let Newel adapt to the new antique market burgeoning all around us, she looked at me as if I'd ut-tered some blasphemy. And in fact, I had—for this was not the way my father conducted business. It was, however, how my sis-ters conducted *my mother*—counseling her from behind the scenes to ignore my suggestions. Keeping her, for their own self-ish reasons, rooted in the past.

My dilemma wasn't merely personal. The shadow of the past was affecting my entire industry. Since the mid-1960s, all the var-ious themes I've mentioned earlier—Hollywood, the Kennedy years, a booming postwar economy, Wilson's glamorization of the auction process, America's new love affair with interior design, along with other sociological, economic, and psychological influ-ences—had converged, until, by the 1970s, the great antiques and decorative arts boom was in high gear. But this time, rather than plutocrats and their dealer-advisors purchasing items for huge private collections, it was *interior designers*—people like Billy Bald-win, Sister Parish, Albert Hadley, Mark Hampton, Mario Buatta and others—who were snapping up antiques for nouveau riche clients seeking to remodel their living spaces. And these design-ers, as well as numerous other people following the cues set by such pivotal magazines as *Architectural Digest* and *House & Garden*, were increasingly buying their material at Christie's and Sotheby's. Why not? The Big Two had become masters at promoting themselves as if they had it all—great inventory, masterful expertise, fantastic prices (*high* if you were a consignor; *low* if you were a buyer)—a charade, moreover, supported by a compliant art press, which breathlessly trumpeted each record sale as if they were an Apollo moon shot. The trade was reeling, the auction houses were handing us our lunches: we had to change, to modernize—but how?

The more I thought about it, the more I came to identify at least one problem: antique dealers themselves. In general, dealers were a tweedy bunch who acted more like academics—each specialized in a narrow field, usually English or French furniture. You'd step into a store and he (or, more rarely, she) would approach you like some baronial lord, acting as if it were still the days when Duveen or Berenson or Belle Greene could spend an entire afternoon discussing antiques. But contemporary buyers—in particular, the interior designers—were time-pressed men and women with multiple clients who needed a place that could serve all their needs at once. These designers—I think once again of Jackie's remarkable eye—were mixing and matching in ways never thought possible before; they needed the equivalent of a high-end antique mall which offered a multitude of historical periods and styles, along with a veritable smorgasbord of accessories. This didn't mean that old-fashioned connoisseurship was out, just that the new antiques dealer had to be ecumenical in taste, encyclopedic in knowledge and New York City-fast in closing deals. How else were we to compete with that combination

stock market, gambling casino, and Wild West bordello they call
the auction trade? I knew of one antiques store perfectly placed
to launch the counterattack — Newel — and one antique dealer
willing to lead it — me.

But I was a would-be reformer without a base of operations.
Newel was not mine; it was under the control of interlopers who
were running it into the ground. The revolution would have to
wait.

Ellis saw my predicament, but with no standing in the family
he could only offer me surreptitious moral support—a shrug
here, a raised eyebrow there, a "hang-in-there-pal" clap on the
shoulder. Marilyn's son Lewis—who was then working part-time
at Newel —also expressed sympathy, but he, too, had no influence. I understood their positions, and didn't feel it was their
place to help fight my battles, but I certainly appreciated their
moral support. Besides, it was my mother who had turned to the
wrong people for support and who didn't realize how deeply she
was hurting me.

Finally, frustrated by the slow erosion of my authority, I gave
serious thought of leaving the family business. And in 1975, I did.
I left Newel.

I spent long afternoons sitting in a small park directly across
from the shop. Like the jilted lover who stands outside his girl-
friend's apartment at night, gazing longingly at her silhouette in
the window, I hung around the area, watching the small trickle of
clients come and go. I hoped that by being near Newel, something—a thought, an inspiration, a brilliant idea—might strike
me. Over and over, I asked my father, *Dad, help me, please: what
should I do?*

I had a client in Dallas who wanted me to set up a Newel-like business down there. Dallas didn't appeal to me, but I wondered if perhaps he might bankroll me if I established a shop in another city—Los Angeles, for example. Assuring Judy I knew what I was doing—a white lie if ever there was one—I flew to L.A. to scout business opportunities. Signs looked good, and I even thought about taking a building on Santa Monica Boulevard. But the lack of parking facilities next to the building dissuaded me (Californians and their cars — you understand). And besides, my heart was in New York.

So back I went. Getting off the plane, I felt lower than ever. My options were bleak: either crawl back to my mother and sisters, or eke out a living in some other business. I didn't know what to do. When I got back to the apartment, Judy informed me that earlier that day, my mother's lawyer had called, asked me to call him back as soon as possible. I telephoned the lawyer the next day. What he told me changed my life.

My mother agreed to give me Newel.

What had happened? My trip to L.A., it seemed, had unintended consequences. Seeing that I was serious about leaving Newel and knowing that Beverly and Marilyn understood nothing about the antiques trade—and moreover, if Ellis were to leave, the company would surely go belly-up—my mother's lawyer sat her down and laid out the facts. If she kept listening to her daughters and kept me away from Newel, she would lose both the family business and her son. In an uncharacteristic burst of clarity, my mother agreed. "Call him," she said.

We met the next day in her apartment. Her terms were these: I take control of Newel, provided that along with normal business expenses, I pay rent, all the utility bills, and property taxes on the building, which she would continue to own. My terms were simple: Beverly and Marilyn are out. I knew at this point I had a strong negotiating position and pressed her hard. I wasn't going to let Newel slip through my fingers.

There were still a few details I wanted nailed down before my mother officially handed the shop to me. Anticipating my future as the proprietor of Newel, I foresaw a need for a loyal and knowledgeable supporter—someone like Ellis, perhaps, but who was willing to take on administrative tasks. My nephew Lewis, as I've mentioned, was working part-time at the firm, as well as serving as an accountant for Coopers & Lybrand. In return for a total, long-term commitment to Newel, I offered him a small percentage of ownership of the company. He accepted.

There is one postscript to the story that occurred prior to my taking possession of the business. One day I walked into Newel while my mother was still its official owner, and I noticed that many objects were missing. Not a lot, maybe forty pieces, but the very cream of the store's inventory. Eventually, I figured out what had happened to the cache. My mother joined her daughters in Montreal, where they established their own antique shop. To the best of my recollection, they called it "Connoisseur." Given the quality of the merchandise, it was an appropriate name.

But I didn't care. Finally, after so many years of frustration and waiting, my dream had come true. I had stepped into my father's shoes to run Newel.

And now I had to go beyond his legacy and make my own mark on the trade.

Chapter Five

Taking It to the Top

Anyone who has worked for years to attain a dream and suddenly finds it within his grasp knows how I felt during this period of my life. Surprise, relief, exhilaration—and a sober awareness of how far I still had to go. My dream, of course, was to vault Newel into the leading ranks of antiques dealers and take on the auction houses at their own game. (My father taught me never to think small!) But to do that, I needed to calm down, take stock and collect myself before entering the fray.

For the next two years, I cemented my relationship with Lewis and, with Ellis' help, resuscitated our rental operations. I hired a new bookkeeper, a woman with the marvelously film-noirish name of Mildred Males, who served Newel for eighteen years until her retirement. In short, like an athlete, I built up strength for the big match. Unfortunately, however, this wasn't Pratt vs. St. Johns—but the competitive antiques business. Where so far, I wasn't making much money.

One problem was Newel's building. The deal with my mother required me to pay all encumbrances on the property—rent, bills, taxes, and so on. I don't remember the exact amount, but it constituted a serious financial burden. My next action, then, was clear: I had to find a new home for Newel, and cut my expenses.

For months I walked the streets of Manhattan, looking for suitable real estate. My needs were particular. In order to lessen Newel's costs, I wanted to rent a space—but one on the east side, around midtown. Just like the Goldberg days, people on the Upper East Side were remodeling their apartments, and I foresaw that they and their interior designers would not travel far to look for antiques. Moreover, I had no intention of establishing myself near other antiques dealers, at that time grouped off Madison Avenue and below Fourteen Street. I wanted Newel to be distinct—not only in style and attitude, but geographically, too. Years before the film *Field of Dreams*, I thought to myself, *if I build it, they will come.*

The place I found was about as unpromising as could be: a remote spot near First Avenue on Fifty-third Street, a half-block from the East River, surrounded by four garages. It wasn't even a single location, but three half-empty buildings that the Bank of North America had recently acquired in a foreclosure action. I selected one space in each building—a basement, a ground floor showroom and a second floor storage area—connected to each other by a Rube Goldberg-like construction of corridors and stairwells. Since it was 1977, and New York real estate was at rock bottom, the bank was desperate to rent the property. So desperate, in fact, that they agreed to an incredible ten-year non-disturbance lease. That meant for at least a decade, nothing short of an earthquake could pry Newel from its new home.

That meant even the controversial Manhattan real estate mogul Harry Macklowe. In 1978, Harry purchased the buildings and immediately began evicting tenants in preparation for a development project. But he couldn't touch me—not for nine years, an eternity for a real estate developer. The disputatious Macklowe huffed and puffed and tried to blow Newel down, but I had the protection of my non-disturbance lease. And to strengthen that protection, I retained the *ne plus ultra* of New York real estate legal firms, Olnick, Boxer, Blumberg, Lane & Troy. Bob Olnick and Leonard Boxer were especially helpful: I remember the afternoon when they perused my lease, then Bob looked up at me and announced: "Bruce, with this document you can get anything you want from Macklowe."

What I wanted was to concentrate Newel in one of the three buildings whose space I occupied—a demand to which Macklowe grudgingly conceded in order to free up the other two buildings for immediate development. But that's not all I got from him: after some tense negotiations, Macklowe agreed to renovate the building to accommodate my needs, which cost him hundreds of thousands of dollars. What's more, he had to pay me a large monthly sum for business interruption. A fantastic deal, if I say so myself, and when the ink had dried on the contract, Newel's new home on Fifty-third Street was a five-floor building, around 50,000 square foot space (five times what I had before), unencumbered by debts. It was the first major deal I'd negotiated as Newel's director, and when I went home to Judy that night, I felt pretty damn good. I knew this was a turning point for Newel, and I felt that my father would have been proud.

Next step: build up inventory. At the time, we had lots of middle-line stuff: average English, so-so French, mediocre chairs, consoles, dining room tables. We also had many non-saleable objects—Elizabethan and Renaissance furniture, for example—that we rented out for stage productions and window displays. Window displays, incidentally, have always formed a large part Newel's business: most up-scale New York stores—Saks, Bergdorf, Polo—used, and continue to use, our material in their windows. But I wanted to sell to designers, the *House & Garden* and *Architectural Digest* crowd who, as I've said, were transforming the look of the American home. So I divested myself of nearly twenty percent of our material, and began frequent jaunts to Europe to replenish our stock with better-quality items. Straining my checkbook, I snapped up anything I could find in Art Nouveau, Art Deco, Biedermeier, and other overlooked styles. Overlooked then, I should say, for today—in large part because of Newel—these styles have become part of the *lingua franca* of interior design.

In truth, with all these trips to the continent, I was actually succumbing to a disease that has afflicted me since my twenties: buying. Or maybe obsession is a better term. But whenever I felt depressed or anxious, I never reached for the scotch or the lithium—I headed off to antiques dealers in London and Paris. But unlike Jack Lemmon tearing apart his greenhouse in *The*

Days of Wine and Roses looking for a liquor bottle, my compulsion was healthy, and nourished the growth of my business. Happy is the man whose addiction is also his profession!

Gradually, I improved Newel's stock. In fact, years before dealers devised the concept of antique shows where sixty to seventy dealers assembled under one roof to display their wares as a way to compete against the auction houses, I was already turning Newel into a one-stop shopping mall for the tasteful, exotic and hard-to-find—an alternative to Christie's and Sotheby's. But designers still weren't beating a path to our door. Our business was growing, but where were the Billy Baldwins and Sister Parishes of this world? How could I reach out to them, let them know where we were, what we had to offer?

Meanwhile, the two big auction houses continued taking a larger share of the antiques trade. The more I watched this phenomenon, the angrier I got. These paddle jockeys were johnnies-come-lately in my field—worse, many of their so-called "experts" possessed only a running knowledge of whatever they happened to be selling that day. They hadn't paid their dues, they never got their hands dirty in the trade. Their whole business, in fact, was more theater than connoisseurship. Yet it was theater with bite, for despite their smoke-and-mirror tactics, the auction firms were slowly supplanting dealers as the center of the antiques market. And this, in turn, meant that where I had to poke through every *marche aux puces* from Portobello to Saint Quen and beyond to find material, people were simply handing Christie's and Sotheby's valuable objects, which, in turn, further strengthened their sales.

As I noted earlier, the rise of the Big Two began in 1958,

when Peter Wilson transformed auctions into social events. And this, in turn, attracted the press, which increasingly devoted more time and column inches to auction house sales. This publicity—this free publicity, I might add—was the sort of exposure dealers had to pay a fortune for in advertising. It was a viscous circle. How could dealers compete with such big-budget behemoths as Christie's and Sotheby's? Or were we doomed to survive off the crumbs from their banquet table?

The answer came from, of all people, Peter Wilson himself. One day in 1980, Wilson, together with Sotheby's auctioneers Robert Woolley and John Marion, entered Newel and nosed around a bit. I knew who they were—and what's more, I saw they were impressed by our inventory. As they left the store, I heard Wilson remark to his confreres, "Why haven't we heard about this place? Why don't they get the word out about themselves?"

Coming from Mr. Auction Promoter himself, the comment stung. But he was right. Why not get the word out about Newel? What's more, why not market the shop with the same rakish glamour that Wilson had brought to the auction world? Why couldn't Newel—and by extension, the whole antiques trade—capture that same *haute monde* sophistication and style?

Through Pratt, I knew a number of top Madison Avenue art directors and executives—George Lois, Len Sirowitz, Steve Horn. I asked them for the most important ingredient of a successful advertising campaign. Their answer: consistency. I then asked myself, what magazine was most read by my target clientele? That was simple: *Architectural Digest*. Then the big question: what did I want Newel ads to look like? Up until then, dealers

usually advertised with images of their showrooms, or a tableau
of tasteful items, as if an accumulation of antiques demonstrated
the depth and quality of their inventory. But my business at that
time had nearly 10,000 objects—most of them first-rate. How
could I advertise that fact without making Newel look like the
Grand Bazaar of Istanbul?

My solution was to combine the theater of auction houses
with my early steeping in Broadway productions: make an individual object, rather than Newel itself, the star of the advertisements. In the way an actor, standing on a near-empty stage, can
mesmerize an audience, or a few choice words by a playwright
can conjure an entire universe, I would base Newel's ads around
the theatrical concept of "less is more." In 1981, I ran the first of
what would become a twenty-year series of once-a-month full-
page advertisements in *Architectural Digest* and other publications.
Each ad depicted a different object, positioned in front of a solid
black backdrop, and highlighted by detailed spotlighting. If normal dealer ads made their antiques look like family photographs,
my images resembled celebrity headshots. And that was the
point—antiques and the decorative arts, I wanted to say, are *sexy,
glamorous, charismatic.*

And intelligent, too. For each ad had a tag-line appearing
over the object intended to tease the imagination. Thus, the ad
depicting an Art Deco chaise said, "For the Rest of Your Life." An
Art Nouveau armchair appeared beneath "For the Price of a
Small House, You Can Own this Extraordinary Chair." A great
number of these whimsies were created by Judy, demonstrating a
heretofore unknown talent for copywriting. The only other text
was a slogan I devised: "The largest and most extraordinary

antiques resource in the world." (Immodest, but true.) And that was it. No age, no price, no description. Like a tuxedo or little black cocktail dress, each object radiated an aura of sleek confidence. They encouraged readers to wonder what kind of place is this Newel? What else do they have?

It worked. The ad campaign grabbed people's attention, especially that of magazine editors and interior designers. In 1984, the Art Director's Club in New York honored Newel with a Merit Award for advertising and design. Over the years, we've received numerous accolades for Newel's advertisements: Burt Manning, the former CEO of J. Walter Thompson, once called the ads "as good as advertising gets" and in 1985, W. Pendleton Tudor, the chairman of *Adweek,* described them as "quality, quality, quality." A great deal of credit must also go to art director Alan Zwiebel, and to Bill Kaufmann, head of Kaufmann Advertising. Newel, the offbeat antiques store in that strange part of town, was suddenly revealing itself to have star quality.

At the time, though, I was too busy to notice our newfound celebrity. In fact, I was hardly in the country. By 1982, I was traveling to Europe every few months, buying like mad. I'd rise early, work alone, stay out twelve to fourteen hours scouring for antiques, hearing all the while my father's voice: *you don't get ahead in this business sitting around reading newspapers.* On one trip I found myself in four hotel rooms in four nights in four different countries—England, France, Denmark, and Sweden. I was driven. I'd bargain hard, but buy on the spot—no indecision, no waffling. Dealers took notice. Soon, I was known as the guy who would buy anything of quality—even the white elephants that dealers thought they'd never sell. Because of Newel's rental business, I could snap up objects that might not be appropriate for private homes: that five foot globe of the world or ten-foot gilt-metal palm tree? If it's stylish, I'll take it!

This also meant I could plunge off the beaten track and, trusting my eye, scoop up styles of antiques other dealers avoided. Italian Directoire, Charles X, Baltic, Russian, French '40s. In Stockholm, a guy tipped me off to a collector seeking to sell his holdings of Swedish Biedermeier. Swedish Biedermeier? Not sure a market for it exists. But hey, if it's stylish, I'll take it!

It was this single-minded passion—this obsession—to probe every nook and cranny of Europe's antique markets that, in 1984, led me to my greatest discovery: the *Normandie* panels. I'll detail this event later; suffice to say, the discovery showered international publicity onto Newel and moved the business into a leadership position in the antiques and decorative arts world. My dream, it seemed, was coming true.

Was I surprised by all this success? Yes and no. Yes, because of its rapidity—as soon as Newel's advertising campaign caught on, it seemed, one good thing followed another. On the other hand, I'd prepared nearly my entire life for this moment. It was as if all the energy I'd pent-up since my teens was released, and like a compressed spring, I leaped into the antiques world. This was my turn now, the opportunity I'd waited years to obtain. It may sound corny—like a line out of the Broadway hit *42nd Street,* one of the many musicals Newel helped decorate—but I somehow knew my destiny was to make Newel a success, and wasn't going to let anything stop me.

More and more celebrities were discovering the shop. Drop into Newel during the mid-1980s, and you might encounter the likes of Barbra Streisand, Rex Harrison, Jane Fonda, Guy de Rothschild, Tricia Nixon, Paloma Picasso, and Bob Guccione. In 1983, when Elizabeth Taylor and Richard Burton starred in a Broadway revival of *Private Lives,* Taylor rented furniture from Newel to adorn her dressing room. When Lee Radziwill wanted some chairs and centerpieces to embellish a quiet dinner in her New York apartment for sister Jackie, she turned to us as well. Major event designers like Robert Isabell and Philip Baloun increasingly came to Newel to find decorations and furnishings for celebrity weddings. In 1988, it was reported in the press that former Master of the Universe Saul Steinberg blew $3 million on the wedding of his daughter Laura to Jonathan Tisch. The services took place at Manhattan's Central Synagogue and featured a chuppa made of four ten-foot brass palm trees—the trees, of course, from Newel—while the reception, held at the Metropolitan Museum's Temple of Dendur, included an additional $250,000 of our Louis XV bronze doré centerpieces and candelabra.

And where money and celebrities go, media exposure is close behind. As early as 1981, Pratt used me in a *New York Times Magazine* ad about successful alumnae. By 1983, trade magazines had begun writing favorable articles about Newel. In 1985, *Architectural Digest* described us as "fantastical," while in 1986 *House & Garden* called me the "Cecil B. DeMille" of antiques. With publicity increasing and many more articles appearing about Newel, I began to consider my public appearance. Not for me the typical "blue blazer" look, and its allusions to English boys' schools favored by so many Anglophile dealers. Instead, I adopted an urbane and sophisticated style—*deshabille* scarves and sweaters, black

tailored suits with perfectly cut pocket squares. Now, I'm not saying I was Paul Newman or anything, only that my personal *GQ*-
look further increased the distance between me and my competitors. And it took me very far indeed from Meyer Newman, who,
standing on the docks of New York at age two, had soiled the
pants of his velvet suit

In 1987, *Architectural Digest* approached me with an astonishing proposal. Editor Paige Rense wanted a photographer to ac-
company me on a buying trip to Europe, recording where I
went, who I bought from, and so on. Friends counseled me to
decline—why tip everyone off to my sources? But no one had
my contacts, interests, or perhaps even my energy. I had, I knew, a
distinctive formula for success no one could duplicate. I told
Paige yes. The result was a fourteen-page, twenty-two-photo-
graph, article in the October 1987, issue of *AD,* which featured
me examining, negotiating over, and purchasing various antiques
from dealers across the continent. It was, needless to say, exquisite
publicity for Newel. And a proud moment of my career.

That year, however, a sad event occurred. Ellis Marks died.
He'd been ill for years with emphysema, but worked at the shop
until the end. With him went a living connection to my father's
early days—his job at Burns & Co., and the founding of Newel.
But more importantly, I lost someone dear to me, someone to
whom I owe more than I can calculate. I suppose one way I paid
him back was by growing and developing Newel; I know he
took great satisfaction in our success. Until the day I retired, I
kept photographs of Ellis and my father in my office. After I retired, I left those photographs (along with an original sign and
skeleton key from our Forty-seventh Street building) at the shop

to inspire Lewis with Newel's legacy.

The beat went on. In 1989, I was featured on the cover of *Connoisseur* magazine, the now-defunct publication edited by Thomas Hoving, the former director of the Metropolitan Museum. There was other coverage, as well—literally hundreds of articles, both national and international, from small trade magazines to the front page of the home section of the *New York Times.* I'd wanted to position Newel at the center of the post-war decorative arts boom, and I'd succeeded. But Newel's good fortune also benefited the entire trade. If nothing else, I demonstrated that antique dealers *could* compete against the auction companies; we could become just as important to interior designers, collectors, and the general public as those black-tie poseurs behind the podium. *And we could do it fairly, without the tricks and gimmicks of the auction trade.*

Newel continued to grow. In 1989, our inventory reached 15,000 objects, making it the largest antiques shop in the world (Today, Newel's inventory totals around 20,000 items.) By virtue of my architectural training at Pratt, I'd designed a system of pallets, dividing each floor of our building into the three levels, tripling our exhibition space. The effect of all those furnishings, *objets d'art,* and knickknacks from so many different eras created an overwhelming visual experience—a kind of controlled chaos that enveloped the visitor. Without planning it, I'd duplicated, in my own fashion, the extravagant interior of one of my early influences—the Brighton Pavilion.

The year 1989 was a high-water mark of my career. For it was then that I organized the "Fantasy Furniture" show at the National Academy of Design. From the beginning I was adamant that the show's title mention Newel. At first the Academy balked—how many museum exhibitions mention the name of a dealer?—but I insisted, and eventually won. The full title of the exhibition—seen in programs, advertisements, and banners hanging from the front of the National Academy on Fifth Avenue—was FANTASY FURNITURE: CELEBRATING 50 YEARS OF NEWEL ART GALLERIES. It was, in short, my way of celebrating my father.

The show's popularity propelled me into the upper ranks of the antiques field. I lectured at many universities, colleges, and museums. For a full year starting in 1991, Chemical Bank used me as a "celebrity spokesman" in print and radio advertisements. I appeared numerous times on Channel 13, New York's public television station, and served as a prime time host for the station's fundraising auction. Then, in 1991, I was the subject of a segment of Robin Leach's *Lifestyles of the Rich and Famous*. After years of serving the rich and famous, I was now identified as one of them.

I'd be lying if I said that this media attention didn't flatter me, but I also recognized Newel's success had made me a symbol of the antiques trade. By highlighting my image and my profession, the media, banking and entertainment worlds were acknowledging that antiques were no longer an exotic backwater, but a vital part of popular culture, with star quality all its own. I'm not in his league, of course, nor did I accomplish this alone (it all started with Jackie, remember), but I think I can say that just as Peter Wilson made the auction world sexy, I helped glamorize the antiques trade.

But I contributed more than appearances. In 1988, Tom Hoving wrote in *Connoisseur* that Newel "had more effect on the way our rooms look now than decorators care to admit." In

1989, one of the country's top designers, the late Mark Hampton, was quoted in *Connoisseur* as saying, "Newel's whole attitude is to defy limitations, the company inspires us to think in areas we haven't." The point is, Newel not only provided designers with a vast inventory of works, but often gave them, and other people, ideas. Or, as New York designer Mario Buatta once said, "Bruce Newman's dedication to the needs of designers, architects, and collectors is thought out to the last detail."

In the late 1990s, I began receiving offers from major auction firms to purchase Newel. I'd never thought about a life outside of the business, but now, in my sixties, I started to consider retiring. Not completely—I'll be involved in antiques until the day I die—but just enough to give me more time with Judy, and to pursue interests outside the antiques world. I hoped to keep Newel in the family, and imagined our daughter Emily, who had started working part-time at Newel, would join Lewis to take over after me. I'd even begun taking her on buying trips to Europe. But she got married, had a child, and was spending less time at the shop. It was clear that child-rearing was her priority. And to be successful in the antiques trade, you must give it everything: time and money, heart and soul, even, at times, mental health and sanity.

Reluctantly, then, around 2000, I thought about selling Newel to outside suitors. At this point, however, Lewis suggested that he purchase the firm. I had no doubt he'd be great for Newel. He'd been with me twenty-seven years, had shown supreme dedication and commitment—and, better yet, had a grasp on the twenty-first-century antiques trade. In 1998, he and

Emily designed Newel's Web site, which *Forbes* magazine claimed was one of the best on the Web. The problem was money: could he meet my purchase price? After some discussions, I agreed to help obtain financing, and on August 1, 2001, I sold him the business.

For years, I rose at 5:15 A.M., reaching Newel by 6:45. Lewis would join me by 7:00, and together we'd work in our window office, drinking coffee, and watching people like Judge Judy and Henry Kissinger walk their dogs down Fifty-third Street. Nowadays, I'm still an early riser, but now it's usually to get onto the golf course. Other than play the links, I travel with Judy, visit Emily and her husband Teddy and my grandchildren Nolan and Phoebe, and try to keep as active as possible.

Several times a year, I go out to the Mt. Carmel Cemetery in Queens. There, at my parents' grave, I relate the latest family news and keep my father up to date about Newel. I imagine him bursting with pride over our accomplishments. Despite my success in the trade, I've always felt that I failed my father by not keeping the family together. Standing there, above the grave, I tell him how hard I tried to work things out, and ask for his understanding. I sense he knows what I went through, and long ago granted me the forgiveness I seek.

But most of all, I thank my father for his guidance, for the knowledge and wisdom he instilled in me. And I ask him for his continuing guidance and wisdom. For it is only now, looking back at age seventy-five that I've begun to appreciate the real similarities and differences between him and me. His was a life in pursuit of a dream—the American Dream of safety and prosperity. Mine has been dedicated to the more personal goal of developing my gifts and responsibilities as a decorative arts connoisseur. My father succeeded. He found his dream.

As for me, I've had my success, too. But my story isn't complete. I still have much to say and teach about the trade. And perhaps it's the beauty of *things,* of age and craftsmanship, that keeps me in the game. For the power of antiques goes beyond home decoration, media coverage or museum exhibitions. It's a mystery that inspires the most active passion of the soul. I was lucky: my father, Ellis, even Jackie Kennedy, conveyed that passion to me. Now it's my turn to pass it along to you.

Part Two

Anecdotes of the Trade

Chapter Six

Barbra, Jane, Sigourney, and McEnroe

At first I thought someone was kidding.

"Bruce," Mildred Males called over Newel's intercom system, "Barbra Streisand on line one."

I went to my office, chuckling to myself, wondering who the prank caller might be. Then a thought made me pause: when Mildred once announced that Jackie Kennedy was on the line, I didn't believe it either—until I picked up the phone.

And indeed, the clipped accent was unmistakable. "As you know, I collect antiques, and I'd like to check out what you've got," the performer declared. "All right if I stop by tomorrow?"

It was not a question. "Of course," I replied, "I'd be happy to show you around." We set a noon appointment. Feeling rather pleased with myself—well, whaddaya know, Barbra Streisand—I hung up, imagining for an instant my new Fifty-third Street building (this was in 1978, and I'd been there about a year) festooned with a banner reading, NEWEL: THE CELEBRITIES' ANTIQUES DEALER. Then I returned to my senses and went back to work

Still, all vanity aside, my fantasy wasn't so wrong. Newel was—and still is—an antiques dealer to the stars. Most top-level dealers have famous clients, of course, but Newel always seemed to attract more than its share. Artists, financiers, politicians, athletes—celebrated individuals of all kinds came through our doors. But perhaps the bulk of our high-profile clients were show business figures—actors, singers, movie and stage directors, designers, as well as others in the industry: people who, I think, felt comfortable with our roots in Broadway and feature films. As far back as the early 1940s, in fact, playwright Lillian Hellman came to Newel, followed a few days later by film star Zasu Pitts—and even Benny Goodman stopped in occasionally.

I want to highlight the fascinating interaction that often occurs between celebrities and antiques. It's a different, more personal view of stars. Just as important, perhaps, it's also a deeper, more nuanced view of the decorative arts.

Since at least the 1920s, celebrities and fine furnishings have gone together. Whether it was silent movies introducing audiences to magnificent objects, Peter Wilson transforming auctions into social events, Jackie Kennedy sparking an interest in interior design—or, more recently, Streisand's own much-publicized collecting—there's something distinctly modern, American even, about the combination of glamour and antiques. Or, to put it another way, the twentieth-century boom in decorative arts owes much of its origin and success to show business. And so, of course, has Newel—from its founding as a Broadway rental business, to the famous clients it serves today.

Now, Barbra didn't just dial Newel at random. She'd called us at the suggestion of a mutual friend, Gary Smith. Gary was then—and is today—a legendary producer of television shows and public events. Together with his partner, the recently retired Dwight Hemion, he has produced everything from presidential galas to political conventions, to television specials featuring such performers as Judy Garland, Paul McCartney, Bing Crosby, Frank Sinatra, Liza Minnelli, and Barbra Streisand. For their efforts, the Smith-Hemion team won a record twenty-four Emmys. Gary even created that illustrious TV show *Hullabaloo*.

I met Gary in 1959, when he came to Newel in search of inspiration. At the time, he was the scenic designer for the *Perry Como Show*, and a rising star in the television industry.

So it wasn't chance that brought Barbra to Newel. She arrived at noon sharp, dressed in the Stealth Celebrity look: untucked shirt, drab jacket, floppy hat, sunglasses. She entered the store, looked around, then asked, "Any place around here I can get a chicken salad sandwich?" She was direct and to the point. I ordered a couple of sandwiches delivered from a deli, then led my guest to the third floor, where we kept our twentieth-century pieces.

Barbra, it turned out, was looking for items for her Central Park West apartment, as well as the Malibu estate she'd purchased in 1974. Our sandwiches arrived and we ate while browsing through aisles filled with Art Nouveau table lamps, seven foot-tall chrome Art Deco *torchières* and French '40s glass and black-lacquered breakfronts.

"Nice place you got here, Bruce," Barbra said. "I like it."

Now, over the years, I've told this story and occasionally a fan of the singer will go goggle-eyed with amazement: you ate chicken salad sandwiches with Barbra Streisand? "Sure," I'd say— "she's a Brooklyn kid, isn't she?" And in truth, for all her diva-ness, Barbra took real pains not to put on airs. She addressed me directly and honestly and before long I ceased to think of her as a star, but as a typical Newel client. We chatted about Gary, the re-cent remodeling work at her Malibu compound and, of course, antiques. Especially her then-current passions, Art Deco and Art Nouveau. Like Jackie, I found she had the regal knack of making people feel comfortable around her—when she wanted to, of course.

But there was something else about her I liked: she knew antiques. She recognized the subtle differences between Art Deco and French '40s, for example, and could discuss such great *ebon-istes* of the period as Ruhlmann, Jean-Michel Frank, and LeLeu. Perhaps I shouldn't have been surprised. Barbra, I knew, had a reputation for thoroughly researching every field she entered, whether it was French eighteenth-century, Art Nouveau, Stickley, or anything else that caught her interest. That dedication and ef-fort is the best—the *only*—way to build a great collection, of course; still, too many people think they can trust their "eye"—or their advisor's eye—and let it go at that. True collectors immerse themselves in their subject—and Barbra was a true collector.

As we ate our sandwiches, she queried me about twentieth-century objects—styles, prices, woods, lacquers, that sort of thing. She seemed eager to make use of my expertise. I was flattered, and answered her questions as a professor might an excited student.

We finished the luncheon tour and Barbra bought several items. Then she kissed me on the cheek. "This was fun, Bruce," she said. "I'll give you a call."

That night, Judy was surprised when I came home with a copy of *Barbra Streisand's Greatest Hits, Volume I*. She had no idea I was such a fan. I didn't either. I still am today.

About three weeks passed, when suddenly I heard Mildred Males' voice over the intercom. "Bruce, Barbra Streisand, line one."

Once again, those familiar nasal tones. "Hi, Bruce. Can you come up to my apartment early tomorrow?" It was not a question.

"I get to work at 6:45, how's that?"

"Yeah, and I'll have cold cereal and yesterday's toast for you. Make it nine."

Nine the next day, I knocked on her door. Now, I've been bowled over by the sheen of an ivory and mother-of-pearl-inlaid Art Deco commode. I've been flabbergasted by the poetic lines of a Hector Guimard armoire. But I was not prepared for the sight of Barbra Streisand in a bathrobe. Nothing too risqué, mind you, just a tight cinch at the waist and a casual décolletage, but enough to catch my breath and cause me to reflect how interesting the antiques profession could be.

If Barbra noticed, or cared, about my reaction, she didn't show it. "Thanks for coming," she said, gesturing me inside her

apartment. She paused a moment to let me absorb its fabulous-
ness, its Barbra-ness, then showed me some furniture in the center of her living room. "Whaddaya think of that?" she asked.

"That" was a three piece gilt Louis XV-style suite consisting
of a love seat and two matching chairs. Or rather, I realized, that's
what she thought they were. Clearing my throat, "Well," I began,
"they're nice, Barbra, but they might not be 'right.'"

"Whaddaya mean?"

I explained that although I hadn't inspected the pieces thoroughly, my gut feeling was that the ensemble was probably made
around 1910–1920 in Italy, when Neapolitan craftsmen were
adept at faking Louis XV furniture.

"Oh," she said. "I see."

I felt sure she'd toss me out. I imagined that she'd summoned me up here, keen to show off her prize possession—only
to have me shoot it down. But instead of the door, she proceeded
to show me the apartment. Or rather, its antiques and decorative
arts. She led me to each piece, told me in great detail where and
when she'd purchased it, and for how much. We looked at everything. Her Tiffany lamps. Her Art Nouveau knick-knacks. Her
French nineteenth-century furniture. Her English mahogany
bed. We even examined her huge hat pin collection she stored in
a dental cabinet, in addition to a brass menorah she kept in a
drawer "for Hanukkah."

Was I a little starstruck? Sure. During my career, several celebrities have shown me their collections, much to my delight, and
the enjoyment of the stars themselves. But I never quite experienced the intensity of Barbra's two-hour tour that morning. She

seemed to really want to show me what she owned. I took it as a compliment; but still, I had to wonder, why she was going through all this trouble?

"I guess I want people to know there's more to me than Hollywood," Barbra explained, as if reading my thoughts.

Of course. How could I forget? I'd long understood that to a celebrity—especially an icon of Streisand's magnitude—antiques can compensate, at least somewhat, for the impersonal burdens of fame. Moreover, since a celebrity's personality is generally constrained by a public image, a tasteful collection of antiques can provide one way to reveal her "true" self without risking box office appeal. No wonder Barbra was so eager to show me her antiques. Perhaps that's why she's been so public about the kind of objects she collects. They make her look human.

And to be sure, antiques can tell a lot about a person. Judging from Barbra's duplex, for example, I could see how her collecting tastes had evolved. In her New York residence, at least, she seemed to be moving from gilt-rich Louis XV toward Art Nouveau and Art Deco—transitioning from glitz to Ritz, you might say. This is a common phenomenon; most decorative arts collectors begin with ornate furniture and then, as their taste matures, gravitate toward cleaner, sparer, more subtle styles.

But my real insight into her personality was yet to come. After showing me nearly every niche and alcove of her apartment, she led me into a corridor that connected to her dressing room. It was a small passageway, no more than ten feet long adjacent to her bedroom. Here, she pointed to a small porcelain Dresden mirror, about twenty by thirty inches, elaborately embellished with cupids, flowers, and ribbons, and decorated in hues of blue and pink. In short, a sweet, but fairly dreadful *objet d'art*. "Whaddaya make of that?" she asked.

"Barbra," I began, as sensitively as I could, "you and I both know that this is not the most . . . beautiful . . . object—"

"I know," she said. "I bought this mirror with the first buck I ever earned singing." She wiped some imaginary dust off the glass. "I keep it here to remind myself of the time when I didn't have any money."

You know that funny privileged feeling you get when someone discloses something personal? When you feel flattered and humble at the same time? I had it then in spades. Standing in that small hallway, before an emblem of Barbra Streisand's early career, I didn't feel as if I were conversing with one of the most influential and accomplished women in America. Call me sentimental, starstruck or clichéd, I don't care. But at that moment, I felt I was in the company of someone who, deep down, felt intense gratitude and humility for her life's fortune.

I have always said, antiques can tell you a lot about a person.

Then, like the pop of a bubble, the moment ended. She led me out of the hallway and, as I waited in her living room, she got herself dressed and called for her car. Less than a hour later, her driver pulled us up in front of Newel.

"Here we go, Bruce," Barbra said in a curt tone, making clear she was in a hurry. She had, it seemed, a luncheon date with Malcolm Forbes. "We'll have to do this again sometime."

I knew we wouldn't, but what the hell. I kissed her cheek, then stepped onto the sidewalk. A moment later, her car merged into traffic and was gone.

I offer that story not only because it involves Hollywood's Great Liberal Spokeswoman, but also because it underscores two points I want to make here about the relationship between celebrities and antiques. The first is that although the public often views entertainers as self-indulgent air-heads with little but good looks and big publicity machines to get them through life—and who's to argue?—when it comes to the decorative arts, many, like Barbra, actually know their stuff.

Rod Stewart, for example, had a good grasp of Art Nouveau. He was no scholar, God knows, and he was assisted by his advisor, Sotheby's twentieth-century decorative arts expert Barbara Deisroth, but he still demonstrated a good running knowledge of the field. (Better yet, he purchased from us some Art Nouveau wall sconces for his "ballroom.") Kenny Rogers exhibited a deep appreciation for wood and wood carving, while Mel Brooks floored me with his knowledge of Art Deco. In fact, the comedian and I once had a spirited conversation about the style at the Louvre des Antiquaires in Paris, where he was shopping with his late wife, Anne Bancroft. "Why are you buying here?" I chided him. "All the best antiques are on Fifty-third Street!"

Jane Fonda was in a class all her own. For one thing, she was sophisticated and knowledgeable enough to mix and match styles: for instance, Victorian English red lacquer with nineteenth-century bamboo. For another, she was a good friend of Newel's who, like Barbra, wasn't above dining with me at the shop—although in Jane's case it was tuna salad sandwiches. This particular meal took place in the early 1990s, right after Jane married Ted Turner. She'd flown into New York for a one-day visit, most of which she spent at Newel.

"I have a bi-i-i-g redecorating job," she complained, as we
settled down to our lunch. "I've got to redo all of Ted's apartments that his former girlfriends decorated." After that, Jane became a regular visitor to Newel, eventually growing very familiar
with our inventory. So familiar in fact, that early one morning,
she rushed into the shop unannounced, exclaiming, "Can't talk!
Got to catch a flight! But before I leave," she continued, jumping
into our elevator, "I've got to get that bamboo mirror I saw up
on the third floor!" I yelled that I'd fetch it for her, but the doors
closed and she vanished, only to reappear minutes later, mirror in
hand. "You know where to bill me!" she shouted, bolting
through the door and into a waiting car.

But perhaps the celebrity whose knowledge most surprised
me was former tennis star and current art dealer, John McEnroe.
John has a keen eye—he and his then-wife Tatum O'Neil once
bought from us, via interior designer Robert Metzger, an exquisite late eighteenth-century Russian desk. Moreover, by virtue of
his SoHo gallery, he grasps the intricacies of the art business. I
especially liked to discuss the auction houses with him. Like
many dealers, he expressed irritation over the practices Christie's
and Sotheby's use to boost auction prices. No wonder we got
along.

My second point is how human antiques can make even the
biggest star look. Take, for instance, my encounter with Sigourney
Weaver. One afternoon just after the 1988 release of her film
Working Girl, the actress dropped by Newel. She'd purchased an
apartment on Sutton Place, she informed me, and wanted it furnished with antiques. I guided her through the various floors of

our building. At one point, she spotted a French Provincial-style desk set beneath some prints hung on a wall. "Hey, that's my office!" she exclaimed. It seemed that the scenic designer for *Working Girl* had seen this particular arrangement at Newel, rented the objects and placed them in the same manner for the office of Sigourney's character, a hard-driving business executive.

The actress visited us twice more, eventually buying a bamboo cabinet, an old Victorian hammock, and a five-foot wide glass-topped table, featuring a carved triple-headed dolphin base. She then invited me to her apartment, where I offered some decorating suggestions and admired the view of the Fifty-ninth Street Bridge looming just outside her living room window.

Cut, as they say in the movies, to a scene five years later. One afternoon, I received a call from Sigourney asking if I could pay her a visit. "Of course," I replied and a couple of days later I stood before her door. Sigourney welcomed me with her megawatt smile and led me into the kitchen. There, she brewed some tea and we conversed about antiques, movies, local politics, and other such matters. Then she got to the point. Motioning toward an object enveloped by a floor-length table cover, she asked "Do you remember that table I bought from Newel a while back? Think maybe I could return it for store credit?"

She had, I recalled, already returned the Victorian hammock. Still, I had no problem with people bringing objects back to Newel. Not only was I certain that I could resell them, but, given the strength of the antiques market, during the time the owner possessed them, their value had increased. I've taken back antiques ten, fifteen years after people have purchased them. Why not? They receive credit based on their purchase price; I get an antique worth a great deal more.

"Certainly," I told Sigourney. "As I recall, you paid around $5,000 to $6,000 for the table."

Sigourney was charming. And having tea with her was delightful. In fact, I was so charmed and delighted that I neglected to lift the cover to examine the table. I mean, would you have done that? A few days later, deliverymen brought the piece to Newel. Only then did I discover that the base was badly disfigured. A dog, no doubt, had gnawed the dolphin heads until they looked like globs of half-chewed chocolate. I'm sure that Sigourney didn't know about the damage, but I had to laugh at myself because I failed to follow my own cardinal rule of checking out a piece.

Which leads me to another story about how antiques can reveal someone's personality. I mentioned before how collectors typically evolve from glitzy furniture to more reserved and "mature" styles. Most collectors that is, for there are always exceptions. Sometime in the 1980s, for example, Alan Funt, creator of TV's *Candid Camera,* visited Newel and came away with, among other items, a pair of French Victorian rosewood chairs, replete with rivers of bronze doré trim. He was so pleased by his purchases and charmed by Newel—I guess its theatrical nature tickled his sense of showmanship—that he insisted on having Judy and me over to his New York apartment for dinner with his wife Marilyn. In one of the few exceptions to my "no fraternization rule," I accepted. Once in his residence, I was amazed at the amount of overwrought, ormolu-thick furniture he possessed. Funt was not an uncultivated man; at one point in his life, he owned a superb collection of Lawrence Alma-Tadema paintings. Unfortunately, Funt was bilked by his accountant for over $1 million (the accountant later committed suicide) and had to sell his paintings at Sotheby's in 1973.

"Alan," I blurted, unable to resist, "your taste is more sophisticated than this, why surround yourself with this gaudy stuff?"

"I'll tell you why, Bruce," he replied, with that patented Funt-twinkle in his eye. "Because it looks like money."

We laughed. But I remember thinking that Mr. Candid Camera revealed more about himself at that moment than any of the unsuspecting people whom he captured on his television show. And it just goes to show you—antiques can tell you a lot about a person.

Chapter Seven

Dustin, Woody, Rex, and Even Nixon

Okay, by now you probably think dealing with famous people is all celebrity buzz and heart-to-heart conversations and un-guarded personal confessions. Well, it can be. But there are also *good practical reasons* why I enjoyed doing business with the no-table and notorious.

To begin with, I generally didn't have to bother with big-egoed decorators who tried to match their expertise against mine. Because of their egos, celebrities often came in alone, or used young, unknown, or moderately talented designers. Once, at a dinner party in the early 1990s, Kenny Rogers—who'd just fin-ished filming another sequel to *The Gambler,* confided to me, "I act about as well as my decorator decorates." I leave you to judge the quality of both.

Another reason I liked selling to celebrities involved time. It irritated me when the "ladies who lunch" crowd would retain Mark Hampton and make a big show of "shopping" for antiques, when their real purpose was to be seen in the company of the late, great designer. By contrast, compelled by their busy schedules, many celebrities made quick buying decisions. It took Alec Baldwin a half-hour to come, see and purchase an Art Deco dining room table. Michael J. Fox instantly assessed and bought a ten-inch silver candlestick. When I observed that the object's base was dented, the actor replied, "Yeah—that's why it's beautiful."

Some years back, Dan Ackroyd and his wife Donna Dixon came in looking for furniture to decorate their Ontario farmhouse. Dan spotted a carved Black Forest bed that featured two enormous bears holding the headboard between their paws, surrounded by numerous other little bears. Dan loved the piece, but feared that Donna, pregnant at the time, might find it threatening. He persuaded her to lie on the bed, whereupon, gazing up at Smokey I & II looming overhead, she exclaimed, "I love it! Sold." (In truth, decorator Craig Wright did most of the house's interior design, including such Newel items as a wrought iron chandelier and a six-foot long 1930s spaceship—which filmmakers had earlier rented from us to use in the 1980 movie *Arthur.*)

Speaking of Black Forest furniture, Disney kingpin Michael Eisner and his wife came to Newel and purchased a number of pieces for his Aspen home, including a stunning eight-and-a-half-foot tall Black Forest grandfather clock adorned with little carved bears. "Do you give discounts?" he asked. I laughed. "You can take the New York kid to the Rockies," I tweaked him, "but the Rockies can't take New York out of the kid."

But perhaps the king of the gotta-have-it-now buyer is playwright and screenwriter Paul Rudnick. Paul is so passionate about Gothic furniture (not surprising, given that he wrote the movie *Addams Family Values*) that when he buys a piece, he has to take it home himself, right then, usually by stuffing it into a taxi. Once, he purchased a large English Gothic Revival wall clock, only to realize it couldn't fit inside a cab. No problem. Paul simply approached some truckers eating lunch on Fifty-third Street and hired them on the spot.

Some celebrities were too anxious to get their hands on antiques. One morning in the mid-1960s, I went to our fourth floor storage facility on Forty-seventh Street, only to find someone had jimmied open the door. Our inventory seemed undamaged and intact, so I returned to Newel's main showroom. I was about to report the incident to the police, when a pasty-faced man walked into the shop and approached me. "We were filming a movie last night and we really wanted those gold ballroom chairs you have in your loft," the man confessed. "So we broke in and took them." He apologized profusely, and I told Andy Warhol—for it was indeed the artist, whose "Factory" studio was then located across the hall from our storage area—that it was okay, as long as he fixed the door. "Okay," he said. "You sure have a lot of nice things," he added.

Still, not every star is so decisive. Take, for example, Woody Allen. In 1978, Allen was filming his first wholly dramatic movie, *Interiors*. One of the film's main characters, Eve, was a successful, but emotionally overwrought, interior designer. In order to reflect Eve's obsession with her career, the film had to exhibit a superb design sense, and I was proud that Allen's art director, Mel Bourne, turned, in part, to Newel. To decorate the set of Eve's bedroom, for example, Mel rented from us a chic bamboo headboard.

Two days later he returned it.

"Woody doesn't like the headboard," Mel explained.

He then chose a fabulous bentwood scroll headboard. Two days later, he returned that.

"Woody doesn't like it," he said.

He then selected a beautiful iron and brass headboard. Two days later, he called again and said, "Woody doesn't like that headboard either. So I suggested to him that he go to Newel and chose the damn thing himself. He's coming at two tomorrow, Bruce. Don't tell anybody and for God's sake don't make a fuss."

The next afternoon, Mel showed up, escorting a small, unhappy looking man clad in a faded jacket, baggy pants, and a floppy hat.

"This doesn't look like the place," Allen declared.

"Woody," Mel assured him, "Newel has over three hundred headboards upstairs."

I took them to the third floor.

"This doesn't look like the place," Allen said, looking around.

"Woody, just wait," pleaded Mel.

I started pulling out headboards, which were lined up in racks and stored along the walls. At that time the floor was not air conditioned and I was soon drenched in sweat. But Allen seemed untroubled by the heat. He never took off his jacket or unbuttoned his shirt.

"No, no, don't like, nope, not that one, no—"

For over an hour, I showed the suddenly less-than-amusing comedian headboard after headboard. He rejected them all. Finally, he threw up his hands and turned to Mel. "See? I told you. This wasn't the place." We went back downstairs, my mood by now foul. No wonder Louise Lasser divorced this guy, I thought. When we reach the door, however, Allen paused and half-nodded at me. "Nice try," he muttered.

What the hell did that mean? Looking back, I can only guess that Allen had some problem with *Interiors* and needed to hold up production for awhile. Or perhaps he is as neurotic and anal retentive as everyone says. Because if you watch *Interiors,* you'll notice that Eve's bedroom contains a chic bamboo headboard—the very first headboard that Mel picked out.

Woody Allen wasn't the only *artiste* who showed an obsessive side at Newel. In 1974, Dustin Hoffman directed a Broadway play called *All Over Town*. The show took place on a single set, with a staircase leading up to imaginary rooms, and to create it, Hoffman's scenic designer, the legendary Oliver Smith, selected from Newel a desk, chair, rocker, end table, and a large Oriental rug. Now, a scenic designer usually just came into the shop, picked the necessary furnishings and had them delivered to rehearsals, whereupon the director would get his or her first glimpse of them. But Hoffman was evidently more hands-on. He asked Oliver to assemble the set at Newel first, and arranged a time when he would come in to examine it.

We cleared a space on the second floor of Newel, and Oliver assembled the scene. Soon, Hoffman bustled into the shop, a harried secretary in tow. He was all business. He ordered the secretary to measure the table, the back of each chair, the rocker seat, while he recorded the figures in a notebook. Oddly, he seemed more concerned with the size of the furniture than its appearance. Meanwhile, Oliver, a thin, well-dressed man—picture a cross between Noel Coward and Fred Astaire—sat on the edge of the desk, smoking a cigarette and regarding Hoffman with a bemused expression.

"Well, Duh-sty," he said languidly, "what do you think?"

"Oliver, it looks terrific." Hoffman snapped shut his notebook. "But there's one problem—my actors aren't getting up the stairs fast enough," he said, glancing around the room as Newel might offer some solution. "What can we do about that?"

"Well, Duh-sty," Oliver drawled, sneaking me a wink. "Perhaps you could make them walk faster?"

Oliver was a great friend of Newel's. Our relationship began around 1957, at the start of his phenomenal eight year run, during which he won eight Tony awards, a record for a scenic designer. During his long career—Oliver died in 1994—he designed hundreds of Broadway plays, including *West Side Story, Guys and Dolls, Sound of Music,* and *Camelot,* in addition to numerous ballets, operas, and movies. For nearly every one of his Broadway productions, Oliver used Newel. One of my favorites was *Lord Pengo*—a 1961 drama starring Charles Boyer that portrayed the life of Joseph Duveen, the illustrious art advisor and dealer whose clients included Henry Frick, William Randolph Hearst, Andrew Mellon, and John D. Rockefeller. For the scenes set in Duveen's living room and office, Oliver selected English Adam-style satinwood furniture (Duveen loved satinwood). And while the play was fairly forgettable, the fact that Newel assisted a master set designer to create scenes involving one of history's greatest art dealers—well, that was, for me, unforgettable. (I still relish, in fact, Oliver's original watercolor sketches of the sets that he gave to me for Christmas in 1961.)

Oliver awed even the most important Broadway figures. I remember the day he and director Mike Nichols were at Newel, discussing some sets for an upcoming play. "How do you feel about it, Mike?" Oliver asked. Nichols look at him and replied, "Oliver, who am I to tell you about design?"

It's because of Oliver that I met Rex Harrison. (Oliver knew everyone.) It happened in 1956, during preparations for the original production of *My Fair Lady,* which he designed. The action called for Rex—playing, of course, the lead character, Professor Henry Higgins—to execute some complicated physical motions on a *recamier,* and he and Oliver came to Newel to select and rehearse on the actual piece. Up, down, up, down, that's right, Rex, turn this way . . . After that visit, Rex who actually lived around the corner from Newel became a regular customer, dropping into the shop maybe fifteen to twenty times over the years and purchasing some wonderful pieces. In 1981, he reprised his role as Professor Higgins. Once again Oliver did the stage design, once again he selected Newel furnishings, once again Rex practiced his movement on a *recamier* inside the shop. Up, down, up, down, that's right, Rex—.

The costumes for both the 1956 and 1981 versions of *Lady* were created by famed photographer and designer Cecil Beaton (he died, however, before the revival opened). Now, Beaton was one of our few clients who actually taught me something about antiques. Before renting a piece, the urbane Englishman would examine it in a mirror: the reflection, he showed me, gave to one's perceptions an extra dimension, a way for one to see an object more objectively. Indeed, Cecil was not the only client who took pains to examine an object from different angles. Paloma Picasso did likewise, especially with a pair of Art Deco chairs she purchased from us. To study their proportions, the jewelry designer—who has a tremendous eye—examined the chairs from every conceivable angle, even to the point of getting on her hands and knees.

One afternoon in the late 1960s, Cecil came to the shop to pick out furnishings for *Coco,* a Broadway musical about Coco Chanel for which he was serving as costume and scenic designer. Cecil was on the fifth floor at Newel, when word came that Liberace was on the ground floor, asking to meet him. Liberace? It seemed that the pianist, a regular visitor to Newel, had come into the shop asking for me, and my secretary had innocently informed him that I was upstairs with Cecil. "With Cecil Beaton? Oh, I must meet him!" Liberace crooned. When Cecil heard who was waiting for him downstairs, his face paled. "Oh, God, no, I do *not* want to meet that awful man."

I agreed to try and distract Liberace long enough for Cecil to escape. I took the elevator to the first floor. There I found the dapper, pleasant fellow wearing an inch-high gold ring shaped in the form of the Eiffel Tower. Before I had a chance to say a word, he exclaimed, "Bruce, you *must* take me to Cecil! I *have* to meet him!" Caught between two insistent aesthetes, I had little choice. I gave in to Liberace's request and agreed to lead him upstairs for a quick hello.

We stepped out of the elevator on the fifth floor to find it deserted. No Cecil. I began to wonder—there was only one elevator and I didn't see him slip down the stairs. Could he have been so distraught about meeting Liberace that he threw himself from the window? Suddenly I heard the pianist exclaim, "Hello there," and turned to see Cecil cowering behind the mirror he'd been using to examine a chair for *Coco*. Discovered, he grudgingly stepped forward and greeted the performer. They had a short conversation, during which Cecil remained as stone-faced as a blackjack dealer. Then, evidently satisfied—if he suspected Cecil's attitude, he didn't let on—Liberace shook hands goodbye. Watching him step onto the elevator, waving and beaming his mischievous grin, Cecil muttered under his breath, "He's *still* an awful man."

Liberace may not have really been an awful man—actually, I found him rather sweet—but I did deal with someone many did consider awful: Claus von Bulow. Or, rather, I dealt with some of his belongings. Von Bulow was accused in the early 1980s of attempting to murder his wife Sunny. He was twice acquitted, and seemed to be so mired in debt that he was forced to offer to Sotheby's property from his Clarendon Court estate in Rhode Island. In one of the rare occasions when I purchased at auction, I bought von Bulow's two eighteenth-century Venetian lacquered bombé commodes. When I examined the pieces at Newel, I discovered in a drawer a pair of women's golf shoes dating from the 1940s—probably Sunny's.

But events involving the commodes took an even stranger turn. In 1989, the movie version of the von Bulow trial, *Reversal of Fortune*, began production. The set designer, Mel Bourne—of *Interiors* fame—came to Newel to look for antiques. In a kind of reversal of reality, Mel found and chose the two Venetian pieces to use in recreating Clarendon Court. It's something a master iro-nist like von Bulow would appreciate: his two commodes, sold to an antique business, returned a few years later as props in a movie recreating their original setting. A case of art imitating reality—or is it the other way around?

As far as other important props in movies—you know the desk that Marlon Brando's Don Corleone sits behind in *Godfather I*? That's right: it came from Newel, a heavily carved, late nine-teenth-century American kneehole desk. When Paramount de-cided to film a sequel, the studio had a small anxious moment when they called us up, hoping we still had the desk in stock. We did, and shipped it out to them. After the release of *Godfather II* in 1974, the production company purchased the desk as a gift for director Francis Ford Coppola.

There are different degrees of celebrity, of course. Some people I dealt with were practically household names. As I men-tioned before, Elizabeth Taylor used Newel furniture to adorn her dressing room during her 1982 Broadway run in *Private Lives*. Hollywood mogul Barry Diller—who has a great decorating eye—once rented a suite of bamboo and Asian furniture to refur-nish a New York hotel room during his stay. Others are mostly known among the social elite—such as former actress and author Brooke Hayward, who's eye and chic sense of style ran the gamut from Bentwood cheval mirrors to Moorish hanging lanterns. Others were celebrated mainly within their own industries: John Loring, the design director for Tiffany, regularly used furnishings and accessories for Tiffany's in-store "table setting" promotions, a great honor for Newel, and a priceless source of publicity. Other clients were famous largely for being themselves—Lee Radziwill, Ivana Trump, Babe Paley, Oprah Winfrey.

Then there was Jim Thompson. Six-foot, six-inch "Big Jim," who, from 1977 to 1991, served four terms as Illinois governor, making him the longest sitting governor in the state's history. He's also an expert on Frank Lloyd Wright—Jim has helped restore several Wright homes in the Midwest—and once owned an antique shop in Chicago. Moreover, he's a good friend of mine, who loves coming to New York with his wife, Jayne, occasionally having dinner with Judy and me at our favorite Italian restaurant, Elio's, and also spending time with other antiques dealers. That's Jim for you: one of the most popular governors in U.S. history and member of the 9/11 Commission, who simply wants to be accepted as a fellow antiques dealer. I can think of no better compliment for my profession.

Jim wasn't the only politician I dealt with. One U.S. senator—who shall remain nameless—visited Newel in search of chairs for his Washington office. "I'd want something good-looking," he requested, "but uncomfortable," I directed him to a pair of nineteenth-century English banker chairs; then, naively, perhaps, asked him why he'd want such unwelcoming furniture. "Because," the legislator explained, "people are always coming to my office looking for favors. I don't want them to feel too comfortable or stay too long."

I'll say it again: you can learn a lot about people—and politics—from antiques.

Keep that point in mind as I tell this last story about Richard Nixon.

Some time after Nixon's election, the interior decorator

Sarah Jackson Doyle came to Newel to find objects for the Oval Office. "The President insists that everything in the office must have American origins." After searching Newel's American floor, Sarah selected two mahogany pedestals. Later, as we were browsing other floors, she discovered a pair of late nineteenth-century argond table lamps. They were beautiful, she exclaimed, exactly what the President would like. There was, however, one problem: the lamps were made overseas—in fact, each lamp bore a small metal tab that read BERLIN, GERMANY. Sarah looked at me. "Do you think you could somehow, maybe, you know—" I understood. By the following day, white enamel had somehow fallen over the telltale insignia, obscuring their origin. And in photographs of the Oval Office, you can see the lamps—in addition to the two pedestals—visible behind the backs and shoulders of *All the President's Men* as they plotted the affairs of the country.

Through Sarah, Newel's relationship with the Nixons continued. She brought Tricia and Pat into the shop around 1970, when Tricia purchased a four-foot horizontal French Louis XV-style bleached mirror. After that, Tricia became a frequent client, whose tastes ran to eighteenth-century French furniture, tinted in pale feminine pinks and whites. She recommended the shop to her sister Julie, who also bought a number of items from us. And where Tricia was formal and reserved—it took her four years to call me "Bruce" instead of "Mr. Newman"—Julie was extremely outgoing. Once, when she purchased a pair of table lamps from us, she threw her arms around me and plastered my cheek with a big kiss. "Oh, David will be so happy," she cooed, referring, of course, to her husband, David Eisenhower.

In the early 1990s, Tricia asked me to come to her New York

apartment. This wasn't unusual, for she'd often invited me to her place to ask for decorating advice. But this trip was about business. Over some glasses of apple juice, Tricia explained that her parents were moving from their townhouse on Manhattan's East Sixty-fifth Street to Saddle River, New Jersey. Could I meet her at their former residence and perhaps purchase some of the items they left behind?

If I expected to find something juicy in the Nixons' belongings—the missing eighteen minutes from the Watergate tapes, perhaps, or a mash note from Madam Nhu—I was disappointed. It was mainly low-end stuff, worth about $5,000 to $6,000. The only items I purchased were a four-foot high Chinese porcelain vase and a pair of seven by two foot wrought iron filigreed gates, which they used to separate their living room from their dining room.

Ten days later, *Penthouse* magazine publisher Bob Guccione bought the gates and placed them behind the front doors of his Upper East Side townhouse. Surprising? Ironic? Not really. To begin with, in the 1980s and 1990s, Bob furnished much of his New York residence with Newel objects. Nor is he an unsophisticated man—with much of the riches he earned from his magazine he purchased a fine art collection, with pieces dating from the sixteenth to twentieth centuries. No, rather—as I hope I've made clear in this book—in passing from the possession of Richard Nixon to Bob Guccione, those filigreed gates underscored the nature of money, celebrityhood and, yes, antiques in America. Everybody wants the emblems of fame, riches, power—and fine interior design. Whether they are an ex-president of the United States, or a purveyor of mass-market erotica.

Newel had dozens of other celebrity clients, of course, most of them not as controversial as those last two: a partial list, would include Yoko Ono, Ralph Lauren, Randolph Hearst, Stanley Marcus (of Neiman Marcus fame), Hal Prince, Sid Bass, Malcolm Forbes, Lamar Hunt, and Barbara Walters. Today, the celebrities still come through the shop's doors—new names and faces I no longer recognize, the next generation of Newel buyers.

Speaking of not recognizing faces, I guess I'll tell one more story. It has nothing to do with me, actually, nor does it have much to do with antiques. But it does, I think, tell us something about the wages of fame.

One afternoon in the mid-1990s, my daughter Emily was working at the front desk when two men approached the entrance and buzzed for admittance. One man was as broad-shouldered as a linebacker with a mean expression, the second, slighter figure was concealing his nose and mouth with a mask; worse, a black van was idling on the street just outside the shop. She was about to refuse the pair entrance, when she suddenly noticed the smaller man's black shoes, white socks, high-water pants—and strange, lunar complexion. Well, of course: Michael Jackson!

She buzzed him in and, accompanied by his bodyguard, the performer wandered through Newel, hardly saying a word. Eventually, he selected five or six silver picture frames. He showed some interest in a life-size nineteenth-century French porcelain sculpture depicting the upper body of a Creole banjo player, but balked at the $25,000 price tag. Then, like the melancholy ghost of some leper king, the pale, shrouded King of Pop, a victim of America's mania for celebrities if ever there was one, drifted quietly from the store.

Chapter Eight

The Normandie Resurfaces

Every born antique dealer knows the thrill of the hunt. The adrenaline-fueled excitement as you search for, and close in on, a valuable item. The battle of wits between you and an object's owner as you negotiate the sale price. The fulfillment you get when you strike a deal and acquire your prize. There's something carnal, erotic, obsessive about this adventure; it combines the exhilaration of sex with the triumph of winning an athletic event. And only dealers who relish the chase, who thrive on the pursuit and capture of beautiful objects, succeed in the antiques profession. For this business is tough, and the secret is not how well a dealer *sells* antiques, but rather how successfully he or she *finds* and *buys* them.

There are different "finds," of course. To discover a Louis XV commode in a New England country auction is unique—but to acquire, an outstanding American Queen Anne highboy from the home of an English nobleman is more satisfying, and better evidence of your skill as a dealer. Then there are the great finds, the historic finds, the discoveries of objects so exquisite they constitute true masterpieces. Dealers dream of such discoveries, not only because of the prestige they bring, but also because we feel it's their responsibility. Each treasure rescued from a dilapidated warehouse, moldy attic, or unknown estate increases the public's knowledge of history, culture and beauty. It's one way we can repay the world of antiques for the delight and pleasure it has given us.

In 1984, I made such a discovery. Through persistence, good timing and skill, I unearthed a spectacular set of objects languishing in obscurity and helped bring them to public attention. The event was noted around the world and marked a high point in my career. I've always considered myself fortunate to find these objects, and over the years, have revealed many details surrounding them. But not all. Now, since I have the time and space, I'm going to relate the complete story of how I discovered, purchased and sold the thirty-two Art Deco panels that originally formed a single mural that decorated an entire wall of the Grand Salon of the French ocean liner *Normandie*. What one expert called "the quintessential decorative arts object of the twentieth century, and one the great antique finds of modern times."

For years, I traveled to England and the Continent searching for antiques. First, I went with my father, afterward, when I took over the business, by myself. As I've mentioned, I'd get up at dawn and work till dusk, scouring the British countryside, every London shop and Parisian flea market, leaving no stone unturned in my pursuit for antiques—and hearing all the time my father's voice: *Don't come back until you find it.*

But I was also hearing something else. By 1982, I'd befriended Parisian dealers to the point that they'd begun offering me tips on where to find good material. And one tip they increasingly mentioned involved a Parisian family named the Benoits. "But of course, Monsieur Newman," they'd say, "you have seen the Benoits, no?" Apparently, the family was an old theatrical clan (to protect their identity, I've changed their name) which over the years amassed an antiques collection *très formidable et excentrique.*

What was to lose? I obtained the number and called the Benoits—and discovered why I'd never heard of them. "No, monsieur, sorry," a man told me over the phone. "We do not sell any of our collection, thank you." Then he hung up.

Ah, that Gallic charm.

I soon forgot about the Benoits and went about buying antiques—so many *marches aux puces,* you understand, so little time. But the following year, 1983, the same rumor came up. "Monsieur Newman, you *must* visit the Benoits," dealers insisted. "They are very eccentric, but their antiques—"

Once again, I called. Once again, the man answered the phone. Once again he declared that his family was not interested in selling. And hung up. All right, I can take a hint.

But the next year, back on the Left Bank, it started once more. As I was finishing business with a dealer on the rue Jacob, the *antiquaire* murmured confidentially, "You have, of course, seen the Benoits?"

Exasperated by this topic by now, I explained that I'd called twice, only to be rebuffed. "Ah, oui," the dealer nodded, "they are like that. *Très privés.* But I know the son Phillipe. I can arrange a visit if you'd like." Sure, I said, why not?

As promised, the dealer called the Benoits and, after recommending me as a major American dealer, persuaded Phillipe to receive me. The dealer then provided directions to the Benoit residence, and I alerted my driver (when overseas, I always hired a car and driver in order to cover more territory in less time). Soon we were motoring past the Bastille and the Paris Opera, traveling for about twenty minutes through a steady rain to a non-descript *quartier* consisting of low-level apartment buildings and warehouses. Following the directions, we turned down a cobblestone street, and came to a weather-beaten stucco arch, leading to an alleyway. The alleyway was too narrow for the car, so I told the driver to wait. I stepped out, opened an umbrella and set off on foot.

The alley was about twenty yards long, lined by warehouses. It was dark, the stormy gloom lit only by a single light at the far end. Not a soul was around. I felt nervous—this wasn't what I expected. How great can this collection be? Is this some sort of trap? The directions led me to an old wooden door. I knocked.

Silence. Then sounds of movement, a muffled, *"Oui, Mama,"* coming from inside, and the door creaked open. "Oui?"

He was a middle-aged man, with sandy-hair and glasses, a Gaulois depending from his lip. *Très français.* I introduced myself—in English, for my French is not great.

Phillipe Benoit peered at me like a Parisian waiter regarding a tourist. Then, grudgingly, he beckoned me in. He was making it clear, I thought, that the only reason he'd permitted entrance into his sanctum sanctorum was because of our mutual friend on the rue Jacob.

"Awfully nice of you to see me, I know this must be a terrible imposition—" I effused, hoping to disarm him. Meanwhile, I took stock of my surroundings. I was standing in a vestibule: to the right stretched a hallway, with rooms branching off—the Benoit's living quarters, I figured. To the left, another hallway, which extended to a larger room—a room, I could see, packed with furniture.

"Come," said Phillipe.

The room was broad, musty smelling and cluttered with objects, some covered by sheets. It looked like no one had ventured back there in years. The first items my eye lighted upon were a set of eighteen bronze trimmed Louis XV dining room chairs. The objects themselves weren't particularly spectacular, but to find an entire set—that intrigued me. Next to the chairs was a Black Forest hat rack, next to that a pair of Art Deco pedestals, next to that—well, there were hundreds of antiques in this room, more than I could take in at once. It was like something out of the final scene of *Citizen Kane*. My reaction was instantaneous. You simply don't find material like this on the open market, I thought—and I've got to buy some of it.

My adrenaline was pumping. I'd spotted my prey and now had to prepare my approach. It wasn't going to be easy. Phillipe was clearly not impressed by my credentials and had already made known his disinterest in doing business. Moreover, every Parisian dealer from Clignancourt to the Louvre des Antiquaires knew the Benoits, but had evidently failed to persuade them to sell. Why did I think I could do better?

Because those dealers were French. And I was American. And as every Frenchman knows, Americans are simple-minded yokels with too much money and too little taste, no?

"Monsieur Benoit," I began, "I know you're not interested in selling, but my company, Newel, has the largest inventory of antiques in America, and buying antiques is in my blood, I have this urge to buy things, anything . . . this console for example—." It was a Charles X satinwood and ebony inlaid console table; quality, but not outstanding. But it would serve as a test. My success or failure in buying it would determine the rest of our relationship.

"I really like this console," I continued, as if overcome with enthusiasm. "And I don't care what I pay for it."

Phillipe's eyebrow cocked. It was, I admit, an unorthodox negotiating tactic. But I had to establish an immediate connection with him. He stared at me for a moment, then said, "Excuse me," and walked toward the residential portion of the building. Pressing his cheek to the door, he knocked. "Mama?" he muttered, then entered the room.

I stood alone, listening to faint voices coming through the wall. Mama, it seemed, was the boss of this operation. I stood surveying untold treasures arrayed before me. Had my offer struck its mark? I could barely restrain my excitement. Finally, the door opened and Phillipe stepped out. He looked embarrassed. "Monsieur Newman, it is not that we need the money, you understand, but—" I knew what was coming. And indeed, the price he quoted hurt—twice what I would normally pay for a piece like this. But what could I do?

"Sold," I said without hesitation, hoping he didn't see me blanch.

I felt foolish, but I'd done it. The rich, easily gulled *American* had achieved entré with the inscrutable Frenchman. Now it was time to go to work.

I bought a pair of nineteenth-century Italian Directoire chairs, a Louis XV bronze trimmed commode, a set of six Charles X dining chairs, in addition to numerous other items. Each time I chose a piece, Phillipe went to confer with "Mama." Each time, he returned with a stomach-sinking price I felt I couldn't, at this point in our dealings, refuse. What the heck, in for a penny, in for a pound, small profits, but I've got the goods.

Besides, I could tell Phillipe was becoming more interested in this rich American. "Perhaps I have something that will interest you, monsieur," he said.

He led me to the back of the storage room. There, on a raised platform were two gold and silver lacquered panels, each roughly five by four feet. Amidst the gloomy surroundings they gleamed like stars—and in fact, placed together they made a dazzling sunburst pattern. I wasn't sure what they were, but two facts struck me: they were Art Deco, and incredibly beautiful. My heart started pounding. Every so often, a dealer gets that gotta have it sensation—gotta have it, no matter what! Looking at these panels, I experienced that urge to a degree I'd never imagined. What magnificent wall decorations these would make!

"How much?" I asked.

"Oh, there are thirty more similar to these," Phillipe answered. Then, after I'd collected my wits, I heard him say, "Let me show you." He produced a photograph of all the panels placed together, forming a single mural. "They come from the ocean liner *Ile de France.*"

"Really?" I said. But I knew better. I'd recognized them from the photo. And I knew at that moment that I'd discovered something fabulous, something monumental: the missing, and long thought to be lost, Art Deco masterpieces originally from the French ocean liner *Normandie.*

It was, in its day, the most romantic vessel on the seas. Called a floating palace, the apotheosis of the great luxury liners that plied the north Atlantic waves, the *Normandie* was constructed at a cost of $60 million and made its maiden voyage in 1935. More than 1,000 feet long, it was the largest passenger ship of its time—and the fastest, able to transit from Le Havre to New York in four days. Its passenger lists included Marlene Dietrich, Cary Grant, Josephine Baker, Jimmy Stewart, and Salvador Dali. But that was the least of its charms. The vessel's interior was a show-case of French decorative arts created by the nation's greatest de-signers and craftsman: murals by Schmied and Jouve, furnishings by Ruhlmann, lighting by Lalique, as well as works of such illus-trious names as Leleu, Subes, Janniot, Daum, Aubusson, and Christolfe.

The pièce de résistance of the ship's adornments was the gold and silver lacquered mural, measuring eigthteen feet high and twenty-six feet wide which embellished an entire wall of the *Normandie's* Grand Salon. Called *Dawn, the Four Winds, and the Sea,* the mural depicted the Roman goddess Aurora in her char-iot, surrounded by mythological figures and representations of the natural elements. It took two masters of the decorative arts, designer Jean Dupas and lacquerer Jean Dunand, three years to complete. Dunand, in fact, developed a new technique for the project, combining crushed eggshells with resin, and applying the mixture onto a lacquered gessoed surface. The result was a gleaming, multi-layered panorama that seemed to glow from within, as if possessed with divine energy. It is, quite simply, the *ne plus ultra* of Art Deco. Or, as I've often said, what the Hall of Mirrors in Versailles is to the Louis XIV period, the *Normandie* mural is to the '30s French style.

The liner's history, however, was short. When the Japanese struck Pearl Harbor, the *Normandie* was in New York and the U.S. seized it for use as a troop ship. Workers stripped the vessel's furnishings and placed them in storage. In February 1942, however, a construction accident caused the ship to catch fire and sink. Over the next two years, the U.S. auctioned the vessel's contents; it returned, however, the Grand Salon mural to the ship's owners, Compagnie Générale Transatlantique. In 1949, CGT installed the panels in the smoking room of another of its liners, the *Ile de France*.

But here, too, the mural did not remain long afloat. In 1959, the *Ile de France* was scrapped, and the panels once again placed in storage. In 1962, they appeared at auction in Le Havre, where Phillipe Benoit's father discovered them. A collector of nautical material, Phillipe's *père* purchased the set for the equivalent of $500. For some reason, he unpacked only two panels, leaving the rest stored in their crates for the next twenty-two years.

"Isn't that interesting?" I replied as Philippe completed his tale. Like a tightrope walker, I was trying not to think too hard about my situation. Here, before my eyes, was part of a sublime artwork, created by two incomparable artists—furthermore, the rest of the mural was intact, in good condition, and stored somewhere nearby. My feelings at this moment were indescribable. I had to exert every measure of self-discipline to keep calm.

Increasing my excitement even more, Philippe volunteered to show me the remaining panels the next day. I explained I was flying back to New York that day, but he promised he'd have the works ready before my flight. That's when I decided not to inquire about the price. It would be a major task to unpack the crates, I figured: let the Benoits do all that work, and perhaps they'd be keener to sell.

I walked to my car. Only then did I realize I was trembling. Those panels—they were the most beautiful things I'd ever seen. I had to have them. But they were not yet in my grasp. Not surprisingly, I had trouble sleeping that night.

The following morning, I returned to the Benoits and Phillipe led me to a storage area situated near the first. Here I found fifteen wooden crates with iron hinges, each crate containing two *Normandie* panels packed back to back. I also found Emile, Phillipe's older brother, a handsome, smartly dressed fellow who had the no-nonsense air of a Parisian banker. Interesting, I thought: Mama had evidently summoned the business side of the family for serious negotiations.

But I wasn't going to negotiate. Not yet. "Look," I began, deliberately glancing at my watch. "It's getting late and I don't want to miss my flight. How much are you asking for these pieces?"

Emile took off his glasses and gave me a hard stare—no

doubt the gesture he used when hammering out terms for a loan. He threw out a six-figure price.

"Oh-la-la!" I exclaimed. "You can't expect—! That's too much for the market—and these panels need lots of restoration— they have to be shipped to New York! All that expense! I can't *possibly* afford that. I'm awfully sorry," I said, collecting my coat. "I hope I haven't wasted your time—" They walked me to my car and, shaking hands, I bid the crestfallen Benoits good-bye and left for the airport.

Sure, I felt bad for leaving so abruptly. But I was prepared to pay twice Emile's offer. Now, however, I knew they were eager to sell and I wanted to keep them on the hook as long as possible. It was a calculated risk, sure—but, that's what made the antiques business so exciting for me!

Two days later, I called Emile from New York. "Something's come up. I have to fly back to London this weekend to look at the furnishings of a manor house. If you'd like to discuss the panels again, I could fly to Paris on Sunday morning and meet you." The "manor house" was a total fabrication; actually, if Emile had said no, I'd've paid his price right there on the phone.

Instead, "*D'accord,*" he replied.

Four days later, I flew directly to Paris and met him. After some coffee and small talk—I wanted to ease my way back into negotiations—I brought up the panels again. Emile offered a slightly better price, I countered with something slightly less; he knocked on Mama's door, conferred for a moment, then returned with a compromise figure. "This is the best we can do." It was something I could live with. "Sold," I said.

Deal done, we relaxed and discussed the necessary financial and shipping arrangements. Then, I gathered my belongings and Emile escorted me to the door. Just before I left that strange residence, however, I glimpsed two eyes peering at me around the corner. I turned, the eyes widened with surprise, then darted back into room.

"*Au revoir, Mama,*" I said. "*Merci.*"

Over the years, people have remarked on my luck in "stumbling" upon the *Normandie* panels. I suppose they're right: I was lucky. But luck is a funny business in the antiques trade. As dealers will tell you, your next visit to a curio shop or country home may reveal some "lost" treasure that you can save from oblivion. But that only looks like luck. In reality, those discoveries are almost always the fruit of hard work. A hunter will spend days stalking his prey or observing his traps—so, too, the antiques huntsman must be patient, dedicated, and persistent. You've got to be out there, day in, day out, to experience that one moment when you're in the right place at the right time. No victor believes in luck, a philosopher once said, and I agree. In the antiques business, as in other areas of life, luck is what happens when preparation meets opportunity.

Capturing an object is only part of a dealer's job. You've got to sell it, too.

Once the panels arrived from Europe, I set up a single row of eight at Newel. But how to market them? Advertise in the press? Contact a museum curator? I was weighing my options when Thomas Hoving, former director of the Metropolitan Museum, and then editor of *Connoisseur* magazine, called. He wanted to interview me for a story about antique dealers and their favorite objects. Ha, I thought, inviting him to Newel that afternoon, do I have a story for you.

Tom arrived just as Alastair Duncan, then head of Christie's twentieth-century Decorative Arts department, and art collector Christopher "Kip" Forbes, son of Malcolm Forbes, were leaving. When Tom remarked on the coincidence, Kip clasped his arm.

"Wait until you see what Bruce has on display."

"It's *unbelievable*," Alastair confirmed. "You've *got* to see it."

I can only wonder what Tom was thinking while the elevator took him to the floor where the panels were displayed. But the moment he saw the panels his mouth dropped. "Wow! These are magnificent! They're like some Renaissance masterpiece!"

"And," I added, "there are three more rows just as spectacular."

Within minutes, Tom was calling *Connoisseur.* "Hold everything! Change the layout! I'm at Newel—Newman's made a fantastic discovery and we're putting it on the cover! The *Normandie* panels rise again!"

And so, the cover of the October 1984, *Connoisseur* featured Dupas and Dunand's tour de force. That was also the end of my questions about publicity. Three days after the issue hit the newsstand, I found a buyer.

It was a rainy afternoon, when two men walked into the shop. I looked at their shabby raincoats and thought, museum curators. But no, one man introduced himself as Michael Smithers (not his real name), a well-known personality in the arts. And although the second man didn't speak, I soon recognized him as an active art collector from an illustrious American family.

"We'd like to see the panels," Smithers said.

I took them upstairs. When they approached the panels, the two men froze, stunned by the spectacle before them. Smithers asked questions about the works, while the other man tried to look casual as he inspected them. But I could tell he was interested. *Very* interested.

The next day, Smithers called. "I can talk my client into buying the panels," he began, then added, "but what's in it for me?"

I figured that the collector was already interested in the works, and I resented Smithers' attempt to get a piece of the action—especially when it was Tom's article that had interested the collector in the first place.

"I already have a major offer from a museum and if your associate is interested, he can call me directly to negotiate," I replied. "But he's got to call me early this evening at my home because I'm making a decision tomorrow."

Now I was on pins and needles as I waited for the call at home. I was bluffing. There was no museum offer. But because of Smithers' attempt to cut himself in on the deal, I knew now that my earlier intuition had been correct. The collector was interested in the panels—and I wanted to play tough, hoping to stoke the heat further.

But by mid-evening he still hadn't called. Had I outwitted myself, I wondered aloud to Judy. These tactics don't work *all* the time.

Just then the phone rang. The caller identified himself as the collector and asked me for the purchase price of the panels. I told him what the fictitious museum supposedly had offered me, and said that if he did better the panels were his. He did do better—but only after I agreed to sign a confidentiality agreement regarding his identity and the purchase price for the mural. It seemed unrealistically simple—but obviously, the collector had a strong desire to buy the panels.

In truth, though, I'd hoped that a museum would have purchased the panels. That's a dealer's ultimate satisfaction—to place an important object in a public institution, where it remains on constant view. The buyer, however, intended to install the mural as the centerpiece in a home that he planned to build. Worse, he didn't even do that—in fact, for whatever reason, he never unpacked the panels. It was the Benoit situation over again, and I began to wonder—was this Art Deco masterwork destined to remain hidden forever?

No, it turned out. In 1993, the unnamed collector was visiting Pittsburgh's Carnegie Museum of Art when (as the story goes) he mentioned to Carnegie officials that he had "some plaster panels" they might use—and proceeded to announce that he would donate the mural to the Carnegie.

With funds provided by a range of donors—including the National Endowment for the Arts, the Florence Gould Foundation, and the Henry L. Hillman Foundation—the Carnegie restored the panels and rebuilt its Scaife Gallery to fit them. Finally, in 1998, the *Normandie*'s mural was unveiled to public admiration. The museum invited me to the gala opening, but business affairs kept me from attending. It didn't matter. I had done my job. I had helped bring a bona fide masterpiece from the obscurity of a musty warehouse in Paris to one of the premier museums in America. And that, as far as I was concerned, was enough.

Who was the buyer, what was the purchase price? Because of my confidentiality agreement, I can't tell you directly. But if you read any of a hundred press accounts about the discovery, you'll find mention of an asking price of $2.5 million. As for the buyer, well, the wall label beside the *Normandie* panel in the Carnegie's Scaife gallery reads "Donated by Frederick R. Koch."

TOP: With my Uncle Sam
in front of my first home,
Brooklyn, 1931.

LEFT: Standing at attention
in Prospect Park,
Brooklyn, 1938.

Erasmus Hall High School track meet with a teammate, 1948.

On the Pratt Institute campus with fellow basketball team members, 1952.

The shop on Forty-seventh Street and Second Avenue, 1975.

My father, Meyer, at the shop, 1970.

My father and I arriving in Brighton, England, on my first buying trip, 1951.

THIS PAGE AND OPPOSITE:
Samples of Newel Art
Galleries' award-winning
advertising campaign.

Announcing an honorary degree to Governor James R. Thompson
at the Pratt Institute commencement, 1984.

The table setting I designed for Tiffany & Company, 1985.

One of the thirty-two lacquered panels
from the ocean liner, *Normandie,* 1984.

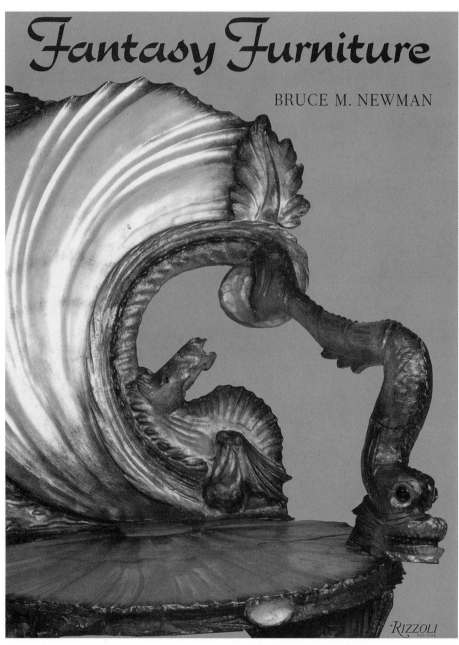

The jacket of *Fantasy Furniture,* published in 1989
by Rizzolli International Publications, Inc.

On the cover:

CONNOISSEUR

OCTOBER 1989 $3.00

THE CIVILIZED WOR...

FANTASY FURNITURE:

Weird, amusing, surreal, elegant, laughable, quirky, bombastic, fun. It's "IN"!

THE LAST GREAT ARBITER OF FASHION

SICILY: DO YOU DARE GO?

PITFALLS OF ART INVESTING

Bruce Newman, the discoverer of fantasy furniture, on the half shell (Venetian, ca. 1885).

0 754794 6
10

Cover of *Connoisseur* magazine, October 1989.

(Photo © Neal Slavin)

Fantasy Furniture publication party at Sotheby's, 1989.
John Marion, Chairman; Robert Woolley, Vice President; and me.

A Chemical Bank ad that appeared throughout 1991 in the
New York Times, the *Wall Street Journal, Barron's,* and the *New York Observer.*

With Mario Buatta and Wilbur Ross
at the World Financial Center's Winter Garden, 1990.

Brooke Hayward, Bob Buck, and me at the dedication of the
Judith and Bruce Newman Gallery at the Brooklyn Museum of Art, 1992.

Nancy and Tom Hoving at a gala honoring me with
Pratt Institute's Founders Award, Plaza Hotel, 1993.

Stanley Marcus, Judy, and me at a
Condé Nast reception in his honor, 1990.

Standing inside the bamboo bed I sold to Jane Fonda, 1993.

Speakers at an awards dinner honoring Paige Rense, 1997.
LEFT TO RIGHT: Tom Shutte, Brendan Gill, Dominick Dunn,
Paige Rense, Paul Goldberger, Aileen Mahle, me, and Steve Florio.

Dinner with Mayor David Dinkins, Plaza Hotel, 1993.

Hosting an award ceremony for Kenneth Feld, Chairman of
Ringling Brothers and Barnum & Bailey Circus
at Madison Square Garden, 1998.

Recipients of honorary degrees from Pratt Institute, May 1997.
LEFT TO RIGHT: Peter Eisenman, Kirk Varnedoe,
Elizabeth Murray, me, and Spike Lee.

Chapter Nine

Fantasy Furniture

There are certain moments when our lives take on extra intensity and clarity. Events sweep us to a summit, or vista-point, and we get an overview of our past and future—the miles we've traveled, the distance still before us, the route we've taken to get where we are. Everything seems well-marked, untroubled by detours and amazingly inevitable, as if following some invisible plan. In that brief space of time, we seem to grasp who and what we are.

A moment like this struck me at the Brighton Pavilion. Another occurred in the aftermath of my father's death. A third transpired with the birth of Emily. I don't know how many such epiphanies God grants us mortals: three in one lifetime seems a privilege. So I consider myself fortunate that, in my later years, I was given another opportunity to comprehend, at least partially, some order and meaning in my life. Like other blessings I've enjoyed in my three-score-and-twelve, I'm grateful to have received it.

The experience I'm talking about was the opening, on September 19, 1989, of my "Fantasy Furniture" exhibition at the New York's National Academy of Design. The show was perhaps *the* high point of my career, one that propelled me into the international ranks of antiques dealers. But it was more than that. It was a deeply personal event that knit together various threads of my life—my father's founding of Newel, my search for manhood, my development as a decorative arts connoisseur. Even more importantly, I think, the show was the capstone of the concept of "Fantasy Furniture," which I'd spent years molding into shape. Together with my 1989 book *Fantasy Furniture,* the exhibition was, in many ways, the culmination of a major part of my life's work.

I'm very proud of "Fantasy Furniture." Over the years, museums, auction houses, and dealers have come to use the term—and the concept behind it—to define a whole genre of antiques. On a personal level, the idea has coalesced to become probably the best reflection of my true self, the Bruce Newman beneath the day-to-day persona: to put it another way, to know Fantasy Furniture is to know me. And along with my beloved Newel, I hope the concept proves my legacy to the world of antiques and the decorative arts.

Having said this, I suppose I should explain what Fantasy Furniture is. I coined the phrase in the late 1980s to describe a class of decorative arts that had previously gone unnoticed by dealers and collectors. The name stuck, but not always on the proper objects. Surf the Internet and you'll find examples of "fantasy furniture" ranging from bookshelves built to resemble ocean waves to armoires painted like something out of an Arthurian fairy-tale.

My Fantasy Furniture consists of superb-quality decorative arts pieces crafted in Europe, the U.S. and Asia roughly from the late eighteenth century to the outbreak of World War I. Their designs are characterized by playfulness, whimsy, cheerfulness, surprise—they are, in short, the products of top artisans setting their imaginations free, unafraid to violate standards of propriety and taste in pursuit of brilliance. "Exuberance is beauty," wrote William Blake, and there's no truer example than Fantasy Furniture.

As I conceived it, the genre consists of several sub-categories: Grotto, Horn and Antler, Grotesque and Mythological, Black Forest, and Belle Epoque; there are also pieces made with unusual materials such as roots, twigs, bamboo, filigreed cast iron, and wicker. Motifs include sea shells, dragons, large birds, bears, nymphs, Egyptian iconography, and other theatrical imagery, often designed in flowing, liquid lines, as if in a stage set by Antonio Gaudí. But words can't really do this furniture justice—even photographs diminish much of its effect. You must experience these objects firsthand to fully appreciate them. As with all fantasy, their power lies in the mind of the beholder.

Another element crucial to Fantasy Furniture is history. I've always suspected that the genre's roots stretch back to the Middle Ages, and the bizarre imagery that monks created in the margins of manuscripts they were copying. By the fifteenth and sixteenth centuries, marginalia-like griffins, eagles, sea dragons, predatory birds, and monstrous and mythological beings had become *de rigueur* in furniture design. These images resurfaced in the late 1700s, when aristocrats and wealthy bourgeois began developing a taste for the wild, fanciful and "Gothic." A taste which furniture makers satisfied, in part, by revisiting the Renaissance's outré imagery. Other motifs derived from the spread of Western civilization across the globe, which increasingly brought Europeans in contact with the strange and exotic cultures of foreign peoples. The father of fantasy décor is, of course, the Prince Regent, whose Brighton Pavilion set the gold standard for ostentation and brazenness. A close second is "Mad" King Ludwig of Bavaria, who in the 1860s and 1870s constructed villas and castles filled with feverishly obsessive interiors complete with grottoes, caverns, and bizarre lighting effects.

Most of the craftsmen who designed Fantasy Furniture are unknown. By the end of the nineteenth century, however, celebrated designers such as Gallé, Bugatti and, in the field of Black Forest furniture, the Swiss-based Trauffer family were creating highly imaginative, tradition-breaking work that combined taste and humor with a dollop of decadence. World War I and the stripped-down, machine-tooled Modernism that followed, effectively ended Fantasy Furniture. Simplicity, not surprise and affectation, became the hallmark of twentieth-century design. People sometimes claim that fantasy returned in the 1960s—to which I say, no way. Nothing in the oeuvre of '60s Pop can compare with the workmanship of nineteenth-century Fantasy Furniture, its materials, forms, the untrammeled spirit of its lines. How could it? The twentieth century was afflicted with soullessness; give me Victorian whimsy over Modernist ideology any time.

But these are the outer characteristics of Fantasy Furniture. To me, the genre possesses an inner measure of experimentation and freedom that resonates with my own sense of self. In a way I can't fully explain, the furniture connects me to a larger, more comprehensive spirit of imagination and life, of joy and movement and dance, without which I simply cannot live.

I discovered this fact during my first visit to Brighton—where, enveloped by the Pavilion's magical tableaux, I realized I could follow my father into the antiques business and still maintain my autonomy. The feeling returned a few years later when, on my first solo buying trip to Europe, I took an "unauthorized" trip to Paris. There, I found a pair of 1860 pine torchère carved in the shape of mincing gargoyles. The figures captivated me; they seemed to whisper, "We're funny, aren't we? Why don't you buy us?" I took up the pieces' challenge and purchased them. It felt exhilarating, as if I was doing my own thing—which, of course, I was. From the very beginning of my passion for Fantasy Furniture, the genre represented something that was my own, some sort of foundation upon which I could build an identity and sense of independence.

Perhaps the gargoyles were smiling at me because they understood this even before I did. For soon, I was searching for pieces just like them—even more fanciful, if possible. And it was possible—I unearthed increasing numbers of fantasy objects, especially when I began traveling to Europe on a regular basis. London, Paris, Sweden, Denmark—any place where dealers had unusual material, or knew where I could find the curious and peculiar. My reputation spread; as I mentioned earlier, I became known as the dealer who'd purchase almost anything. Huge birdcages, Moorish arches, oversize blackamoor figures—I bought them not only for their "rentability," but because they affected me in some mysterious manner, a manner I can only describe as love.

Can someone fall in love with antiques? Why not? (Actually, no true antiques dealer would even ask the question—for us, the answer is self-evidently yes.) I felt drawn to fantasy objects, enjoyed their company, preferred their spirited romanticism to more "down-to-earth" antiques. I'd stare at a German six-foot-tall painted pine figure of Mephistopheles and wonder—who owned this? Why was it made? Like some love-struck swain, I wanted to know what my pieces were like before they met me. I'm not saying, of course, that my appreciation of a Texas steerhorn settee or a Scandinavian cork-veneered armchair equaled what I felt for Judy and Emily—it's just that Fantasy Furniture gave me a profound sense of inner satisfaction no other antiques duplicated.

Recently, a writer I know made an intriguing observation about Fantasy Furniture. He suggested that its loose, flowing lines, its humor and eclecticism, provides a feminine counterpart to solid, stolid, traditionally masculine styles like Chippendale and Regency. This made sense and seemed to explain, in part, why I love the genre. I remember always calling Judy from Europe telling her about the new Fantasy pieces I'd discovered, as excited as if I'd met new members of my family. And, in a way, I had.

But my passion for Fantasy Furniture runs deeper than that. The sense of creativity, imagination and history these objects possess represent something larger than myself. I'm not a particularly religious man. But I do believe in some sort of transcendent power, a world spirit, which flows through life, permeating and enveloping us. In the presence of Fantasy Furniture, I feel that spirit.

By 1988, I'd amassed over 1,000 examples of unusual and bizarre objects. I began to realize that they formed an identifiable genre. But what to call it? I originally thought of "Quality Camp." But "Camp" has pejorative connotations—irony, artificial passions, aesthetic staleness. To me, the furniture was as vibrant and alive as the day it was made. That's when I thought of Brighton. What was the element that so attracted me to Prinny's fun-palace? Fantasy. The power of the imagination to transform the normal strictures of reality into a realm of vitality and wonder that can transform worlds, people, individuals. Not Camp—but Fantasy! So the name was born: Fantasy Furniture.

At this time, my career was still enjoying publicity from my discovery of the *Normandie* panels, in addition to the twenty-page photo spread about my hunt for antiques that ran in *Architectural Digest* in 1987. I knew success would prove fleeting unless I found another project to keep me in the public eye. Why not, I thought, organize a public display of Fantasy Furniture? Rent, say, some booths at a high-end antiques fair and exhibit forty of my best pieces? Wow the crowds, reap some publicity, make some sales, form new contacts.

But what was I thinking? I never did antiques fairs. Created by dealers to compete with Christie's and Sotheby's, fairs are essentially glitzy malls taking place in London, Palm Beach, or Manhattan's Park Avenue Armory. Go to one and you'll find booth after booth of dealers standing around like vendors in a souk. My approach to the antiques business was to separate myself from my competitors. I didn't want to become "one of the boys," standing around waiting for Henry Kravis to enter my booth and buy a trinket. Besides, Newel—with its multiple floors of eclectic inventory representing centuries of the decorative arts—was its own antiques fair.

A book, then. Entitled *Fantasy Furniture,* featuring about 200 top-quality pieces. I mentioned the idea to Alastair Duncan, who nearly burst with excitement. Even better, he contacted representatives from two publishing firms that specialized in art books: Abrams and Rizzoli Books. Although both firms expressed interest, I opted to go with Rizzoli. The company gave me an advance, I hired a photographer and started producing my opus.

I'm particularly grateful to Robert Janjigian, my editor at Rizzoli, for allowing me to oversee *Fantasy Furniture*'s design — from the actual choice of objects to the manner in which the photographs appeared on the page. I enjoyed other assistance as well. Tom Hoving wrote the Foreword, while other celebrated collectors and experts further endorsed the book by composing short introductions to each chapter. Interior designer Sister Parish wrote about Grotesque and Mythological furniture; the other writers were the famous Art Deco artist Erté (Grotto); department store king Stanley Marcus (Horn and Antler); author and Metropolitan Museum lecturer Marvin Schwartz (Black Forest); Tiffany's director of design John Loring (Belle Epoque); and Sotheby's chairman John Marion ("Materials"). Condé Nast editorial advisor Leo Lerman contributed the Afterword. For his part, Alastair proved an enormous help with his extensive research and encouragement.

The book was a 200-page extravaganza, lavishly illustrated with hundreds of full-color photographs. Not only did Rizzoli published it in September 1989, with a good-size print run in English and Italian, but Flammarion published it in French. Out of the seventy books that Rizzoli released that fall, *Fantasy Furniture* received the most requests from the media for review copies. The book proved a great success. *Time* magazine chose it as a "best pick" for Christmas 1989, while the *New York Times* listed it as a great "last minute Christmas gift." *House & Garden* gave copies of *Fantasy Furniture* to its top clients as a holiday present. Gene Schalit gave it a rave review on NBC's *Today Show*.

More excitement was to come. In the early summer of 1989, I had lunch with Bob Buck, then-director of the Brooklyn Museum. Bob and I knew each other well: among our dealings in the decorative arts world, we both served on the board of the Pratt Institute. During our conversation, I mentioned that my book *Fantasy Furniture* would be released shortly, and he became interested. Perhaps, he suggested, I could drop by the BMA and show some transparencies of the objects to him and Diane Pilgrim, the museum's curator of decorative arts? "Of course," I replied—and a few days later I drove out to my old stomping ground along Eastern Parkway. Bob and Diane met me, and before long they were oooh-ing and ahhh-ing over my slides of floriform walnut plant stands, Florentine peacock-shaped armchairs and other unique objects. "We've got to have a show of these!" Bob exclaimed.

Everything was going well—we'd actually begun discussing the outlines of a Fantasy Furniture exhibition at the BMA—when Bob and Diane paused. It seemed they'd run across the transparency showing what I called King Edward VII's "love chair." Used by the future English king in the most famous Parisian bordello, *Chapanias,* it was a custom-made 1890s rococo contraption, fitted with gilt bronze stirrups, carved handgrips and

two levels of padded cushions—ideal for a royal rake to dally
with multiple partners at once. The piece troubled Bob and Diane. Children and school groups visit the museum, they demurred—how could they explain to parents and teachers why
the BMA was exhibiting something like this? Call me cynical,
but I didn't share their concerns that a nineteenth-century antique might corrupt the innocence of children—that's what
MTV is for, isn't it?—and besides, I loved the piece; it was the fo-
cal point of my fantasy collection and a surefire publicity grabber.
Disappointed, I told Bob and Diane I'd have to think about their
objections to the love chair—and whether I wanted to mount a
show without it. (Little did I know what future trouble I'd have
with the BMA—in particular, Buck's successor, Arnold Lehman—over the issue of Fantasy Furniture!)

By coincidence, that night I had dinner with Wilbur Ross,
then-chairman of the National Academy of Design, Manhattan's
180-year-old fine arts museum, school and artists association,
located on upper Fifth Avenue. I told Wilbur about my experience at the BMA and he suggested I mount a Fantasy Furniture
exhibition at his institution. And to get matters rolling, he promised to set up a meeting with the Academy's director, John
Dobkin. Over the next few days, the idea of a Fantasy Furniture
exhibition began to loom in my mind. By the time I met John
Dobkin, I'd conceived of a plan for a big, extravagant show, one
that required a lot of the Academy's space and, of course, included
the love chair. Moreover, it had a title that later proved controversial. A little to my surprise, I must admit, John loved the idea.
Even more astonishing, he asked if I could put the show together
by September 1989.

Sure, I said, swallowing hard. The next day, I burrowed into the work. I called contacts I had on the board of New York's Chemical Bank—Newel had been a client of the bank since 1939—and they agreed to underwrite part of the show. With this money, I retained renowned event designer and frequent Newel client Philip Baloun. Soon, Philip and I were designing everything from display pedestals and lighting effects to pillars, columns, and wall-hangings to decorate the Academy's galleries. Meanwhile, I spent hours organizing a benefit committee for the show: people who agreed to participate included Mrs. Randolph Hearst, Nan Kempner, Mrs. Ronald Lauder, and Mrs. William Sarnoff. I also supervised preparations for the gala dinner. All together it was, without doubt, the largest undertaking of my career. And the most rewarding.

After a month of design preparation and another month to create and install the exhibition, opening night arrived. It was a star-studded event. The honorary chair was Erté, co-chairs were Lee Radziwill, Rex Harrison, Kip Forbes, and New York socialites Catie Marron and Fernanda Niven. The guests included other luminaries of New York's social and philanthropic circles such as Milton and Carroll Petrie, Jerome Zipkin, and Jean Suffern-Tailer. Bob Buck and Tom Hoving were there, as were the *beau monde* of the design world, including Mark Hampton, Robert Metzger, and Mario Buatta.

The dinner, held in the Academy's third floor Stone Room, overflowed with beauty, wit, and style. To enhance the affair, I situated at each table some of my best "fantasy centerpieces"— four-foot-tall blackamoor figures, porcelain vases made in the form of fresh-cut daisies, Art Nouveau dancing figures and other exotic objects, all decorated with large arrays of flowers.

As for the show itself, well, permit me to give you a tour. Approaching the Academy's Beaux Arts mansion from Fifth Avenue, the first thing you saw were two purple banners emblazoned with gold letters that read: FANTASY FURNITURE: THE FIRST 50 YEARS OF THE NEWEL ART GALLERIES. As you might imagine, that raised a few hackles—how many museum exhibitions commemorate a commercial dealer, especially one still in operation? But from the moment I conceived this show, I wanted to draw public attention not only to Fantasy Furniture, but to the legacy of my father, as well. For weeks afterward, I heard grumbling about what I'd done—some people complained I had soiled the purity of the Academy by mixing art and commerce (others even felt that a decorative arts exhibition did not belong at the "fine art" museum in the first place). I didn't care—as one New York critic wrote, Newel was "no ordinary gallery, but an institution." Besides, I knew I'd created something spectacular, something New Yorkers would love. For if there's one thing this city appreciates—it's a show.

And what a show! Just inside the Academy's front doors, two ten-foot red and gold lacquered herons stood on either side of a seven-foot-tall Regency birdcage, made of filigreed bamboo with a pagoda-shaped top. Surrounding the birdcage were plush cushions and carved panels featuring ornate latticework, while on the wall behind hung a ten by twelve-foot nineteenth-century red silk carpet, decorated with gold embroidery forming intricate Chinese patterns. Adding to the ambience were ten-foot horizontal red and gold lacquered dragons, undulating overhead. The effect was startling, spectacular. I'm in the Brighton Pavilion, I hoped visitors would think, half-expecting to see Prinny himself descend the Academy's staircase.

But that was just the beginning. Past the birdcage, you moved up the staircase, beneath a ten-foot wooden heron, lacquered brown with gold highlights, which hung from the ceiling. The heron was a sort of an archway, under which visitors passed to access the sights beyond. Like a child listening to a gripping story, I wanted people to feel delight and astonishment and wonder what's going to happen next?

"Next" was a twelve-foot square open area adorned in each corner by four eight-foot carved pearwood nymphs, festooned together with garlands of flowers and ivy vines. And in the middle of this verdant opulence was none other than Edward VII's love chair, preening in all its salacious and libertine glory, attracting all the attention I knew it would.

Beyond the *siège de scandale,* the exhibition moved into a series of galleries, each gallery designed to reflect a chapter of *Fantasy Furniture.* The Belle Epoque room, for example, was a gigantic Valentine's Day card featuring four oversize gilt-carved putti hanging over a French Victorian cradle swaddled in thick red drapery, the whole scene positioned in front of an ornately carved ten-foot mirror ornamented with flying cupids. There was also a six-foot high mahogany mantle in the style of Hector Guimard, bedecked in a firefly motif, in addition to a set of towering blackamoors, and a tall-case Art Nouveau clock, carved with a reclining woodland nymph.

Belle Epoque led to the Gothic chamber, where, *à la* Mad King Ludwig, the walls were painted sky-blue with clouds, and the space filled with Grotto furniture—rough-hewn chairs, tables, tripod jewelry caskets and other pieces, decorated with dolphins, tridents, seashells, and sea horses, then silver-leafed and covered with a gilt metallic wash until they gleamed like the halls of Atlantis. After that came the Materials room, which featured such unique objects as a wrought-iron bench cast to simulate twigs, a bentwood plant stand, and a Japanese-inspired fire screen made of gnarled and twisted roots.

Retracing their steps, visitors crossed back through the area displaying the love chair, then entered a room measuring forty by twenty feet, tented with black canvas. Here, in near total darkness, spotlights illuminated a phantasmagoria of mincing satyrs, exhibitionistic peacocks, twisting Oriental dragons, and other Grotesque and Mythological objects—including my two mocking gargoyles, the fantasy pieces that started it all.

The sense of dreamy surrealism deepened as people moved from the darkness of the Mythological room to a full-fledged forest. Here, Texas met Germany in a display that combined Horn and Antler and Black Forest objects. Bears affixed to table legs or rearing up from the backs of chairs peered through the potted and artificial trees, while a twelve-light chandelier made of stag and steer horns hung over "trophy" furniture and accessories incorporating antlers, horns, hooves, and carved animal heads. The effect of the room—of the entire show, in fact—was jarring and playful, as if the Academy, and its visitors, had been transported to a wonderland of sprites and goblins, curious animals, mischievous demons, and other unnamable denizens of the imagination. The world, in short, of fantasy—and Fantasy Furniture.

The gala was a huge hit. During the evening, Tom Hoving shook my hand. "This is one of the most exciting decorative arts shows I've ever seen," he enthused. "If I was still director of the Met, I'd've put it there." A somewhat chagrined Bob Buck sidled up to me and murmured, "I have to admit, I'm sorry we didn't do the exhibition." (On the other hand, I thought, it isn't everyone who can truthfully say they've been "banned in Brooklyn.")

The show went on until mid-October, proving popular among the public and press alike. Critics raved. The *New York Times* ran a Home Section cover story about the exhibition, featuring a photograph of me in the Grotto Room; England's *The Antique Collector* described it as a "landmark show," while *Vogue Decoration* called it "memorable."

The show's effects extended beyond New York. I've already mentioned how "Fantasy Furniture" became a well-known category used by decorative arts experts around the world. The two most popular classes of Fantasy Furniture—Black Forest and Grotto—exploded in value. Call it the sincerest form of flattery, but furniture makers in Asia soon began cranking out imitation pieces utilizing bear and oceanic imagery. On another level, by writing a book, creating an entire genre of decorative arts, and mounting a world-class museum show, I once again stretched the boundaries of what the public expected from antiques dealers. My accomplishments were personal triumphs, to be sure, but they nevertheless boosted the image of dealers everywhere, and helped us in our eternal battle with the auction firms.

Speaking of personal triumphs, some time during the opening night festivities, I left the Academy and walked across Fifth Avenue. I looked at the banners displaying Newel's name and felt my heart swell. It wasn't so long ago, I reflected, that I'd stood outside of Newel, banished from the business by my mother and sisters, feeling increasing despair as I wondered where my future was heading. Now, fifteen years later, I was looking at a full-scale testament to my love for Fantasy Furniture and for Newel. If only I could go back to comfort that younger Bruce Newman, offer him a vision of tonight's gala, the show that inspired it and how my fortunes turned out.

There are moments when we seem to sense the grand order of our lives, how our successes and failures combine to form the unique pattern we call our "self." Earlier in the evening, just before the Academy's doors opened and the guests arrived, I stood in the Mythological room for a brief respite. The room's rectangular shape reminded me of Newel's original location on East Forty-seventh Street, and I thought back to those days. I recalled how frightened I was when my parents took antiques from our home to start their new business, how they laid those objects out on a long, narrow table for sale. It seemed an incredible journey, from that single table to a world-class museum show. That's why I insisted that the exhibition's complete title mention Newel, for I envisioned it as a celebration of the business, its growth and development, its importance in my life.

Surrounded by the darkness of that tented room, I seemed to see the faces and objects of nearly fifty years float before me. I saw Ellis, showing me the secrets of how furniture is made; I visualized the coiled serpent lamp that so captured my childhood imagination. I was once again a teenager, thrilled by the exhibits in the Brooklyn Museum and the glamorous sets of the twenty-five-cent movies I saw at the local cinema—and then a young man, provoking my teachers at Pratt with my passion for antiques. The Brighton Pavilion, Jackie Kennedy, and other celebrities, my buying trips to Europe and the *Normandie* panels, Judy, Emily—all the highpoints of my life came back like friends congratulating me on my success. Low points came, as well—family conflicts and other disappointments. And though I tried to push them away, I understood that they, too, helped form the story of my life.

Most of all, I thought of my father. For at its deepest level, this exhibition was a commemoration of him, his life, how he founded Newel, how he guided me into the business. And how much I loved him. How many sons have the fortune to express so magnificently their love for their father? Standing in the dark, I sensed him beside me, taking in all the evening's glamour with intense satisfaction. Satisfaction not only in how successful Newel turned out, but in the kind of man his son grew to be. And at that moment, he seemed to address me, saying, finally, the words I'd so desperately wanted to hear from him. You've done well, son, my father said. You've made me very proud. Turning toward his invisible presence, I nodded. Thank you.

Then, straightening my bow tie, I went to join my guests.

Chapter Ten

The Royal Copycat

A man sits down to write his memoirs, it seems to me, for three basic reasons: to put his experiences into some kind of order, to offer readers his hard-earned wisdom and, lastly, to tell his side of controversial events in his life. Now, at this point in my memoirs, I've pretty much completed the first task, and I'll begin the second in a moment. But here, in this present chapter, I want to "set the record straight" about a matter that has nettled me for years.

It involves my book *Fantasy Furniture,* which, as you know, was published in 1989, and an all-too-similar book published by an Englishman in the mid-1990s. Now, I'll be the first to admit that this is not a huge issue—nothing like my hunt for the *Normandie* panels or my vexations with the auction houses—but, as I mentioned, it's a controversy I want to straighten out, once and for all. Notice I don't say I want to "settle an old score" against the offending book and its author. For the moral of this tale involves a personal victory I achieved in overcoming a tempting, but almost certainly ruinous, impulse for vindication and revenge.

Allow me to explain. I was reading the November 1996 issue of *House & Garden* magazine, when I ran across an article lauding a recently published book entitled, of all things, *Extraordinary Furniture*. Isn't that interesting, I thought. Even more interesting was a photograph from the book that *HG* had reproduced for its article: a Grotto-style console and mirror that was a dead ringer for the pieces I featured in *Fantasy Furniture*. The photograph even contained the sky-blue background I'd devised for the Grotto room in the Fantasy Furniture show.

More interesting yet was the author of *Extraordinary Furniture:* Viscount David Linley, the son of Great Britain's Lord Snowdon and Princess Margaret—making him the Queen's nephew and eleventh in line for the Royal Crown. A fixture of England's high-society set, Linley was, by all accounts, a decent fellow who, since 1985, had designed and manufactured his own line of furniture and accessories, with a store located on London's fashionable Pimlico Road. Good taste, impeccable quality, solid reputation, that sort of thing. Unfortunately, it seemed he'd been a bit careless with his new book.

How careless I soon discovered. I acquired a copy and was astonished to find that the author had organized it into a number of sections focused on certain "extraordinary" styles of furniture—among them, Horn and Antler, Papier Mâché, Bamboo, and Black Forest. Ring a bell? I thought so, too. Although these areas of the decorative arts were just a small part of his book, the

Grotto section gave me a particular case of déjà vu. It seemed that the Viscount had chosen to feature several pieces virtually identical to those which appeared in *Fantasy;* moreover, some of the photographs he selected to illustrate these objects seemed remarkably close to those that appeared in my book. For example, in *Fantasy* I featured a two-seated chair commonly known as a "tête-à-tête," but which I called an "S-shaped confidante;" in *Extraordinary,* Linley presents a near-identical piece photographed from exactly the same perspective which he also calls an "S-shaped confidante." Coincidence? I wonder.

But that was the least of *Extraordinary*'s apparent "borrowings." As I read his prose, I thought, My, this sounds familiar. For sure enough, Linley repeated, or reworked in the most cursory manner, phrases, descriptive concepts and, at times, exact words which had originally appeared in over twenty passages of *Fantasy.*

I was, you might say, annoyed. Maybe if Linley had credited my book with inspiring his own, or if he'd acknowledged that my work had served as a source for his research, I might have been mollified. No, come to think of it, I would have been honored—after all, *Extraordinary* was a top-quality book about topics close to my heart. But of the fifty-three sources listed by the Royal Nephew in his tome's bibliography, *Fantasy* was nowhere to be found. How could this be? My annoyance grew to pique when I made an initial, friendly, phone call to the Linley people to ask about the omission. "David has never even seen your book," I was told in no uncertain terms.

Right. And the sun never sets on the British Empire.

The nerve of this guy, I thought. I created the field of Fantasy Furniture. I worked a year and a half to write the definitive book on the subject. And he comes along and uses my research without giving my book so much as a credit line.

Lest you think I was overreacting to Linley's opus, let me indulge your patience by offering some additional examples of what I consider to be borrowings from *Fantasy Furniture*. That way, you can judge for yourself. (I've put the similarities between our two books in italics for your comparison.)

Exhibit A comes from page 59 of *Fantasy:*

> *In the 18th century* the aristocracy in England and Europe were caught up in a craze for *folly* building
> . . .

Now turn to this passage from page 166 of *Extraordinary Furniture:*

> *By the end of the 18th century* indoor and outdoor *grottoes* were as much a feature of the grand house as *follies* . . .

Or take this bit of borrowed research, found on page 80 of *Fantasy,* where I introduce Horn and Antler furniture. "*Revived interest,*" in the furniture, "came in the *early nineteenth century,*" I write, then continue:

> Its use only became widespread around 1800. *Sheraton's Cabinet Dictionary of 1803 showed an adjustable hunting chair whose legs were fashioned from single*

antlers. It was described as "a temporary resting place for one that is *fatigued, as hunters generally are.*

I direct your attention now to page 162 of *Extraordinary:*

> *By the early 19thcentury* horn furniture... *began to be increasingly popular.* The idea soon crossed the Channel and in *1803 Sheraton included a horn-legged chair in his Cabinet Dictionary, describing it as an ideal meeting place "for one that is fatigued, as hunters generally are.*

On page 84 of *Fantasy,* I observe that the "protruding sharp ends" of Horn and Antler furniture were "capped with acorn finials to prevent flesh wounds and *impaled* clothing." Echoing my point almost exactly, Linely's book states on page 163, that "jagged prongs of horn are woven together at the front, to save the chairs' users from becoming *impaled."*

Turning to Papier-Mâché furniture, I note, on page 189 of *Fantasy.* that:

> The undecorated papier-mâché blanks were now ready to be "japanned" with a high-gloss paint that *imitated . . . the oriental technique of lacquering . . .*

Linley appears to agree, for on page 160 of *Extraordinary,* we read*:*

The material was usually finished by japanning and
painting it in imitation of oriental lacquer . . .

To seal my argument, I'd like to cite just one more passage,
this one involving a discussion of bamboo. On page 179 of *Fantasy,* I mention that the "west's captivation with the orient
reached it's height in the 1750s," adding that

by the 1790s this cult had *faded,* but it was *revived
abruptly* by the Prince Regent's creation of the
Brighton Pavilion.

For it's part, *Extraordinary,* on page 152, also points out that
Prinny acquired the Brighton Pavilion in the late eighteenth
century—but then, in a remarkable echo of my point about "ori-
entalism," adds:

Rooms decorated in "Chinese style" had recently
enjoyed a heyday but by this time the fashion had
faded and the decoration of the Royal Pavilion
marked a *resurgence* of fascination with the arts of
the East . . .

When I pointed these "coincidences" to people, a few just
shrugged. The passages weren't direct copies, they noted, and besides, there are only so many words you can use to describe
something. But that was my whole point! I created this field of
"unusual" furniture six years earlier. It defied logic to believe that
anyone could write about it and not be aware of, or give credit

to, my work. (Interestingly, in its review of *Extraordinary,* the *Maine Antiques Digest*—an important trade publication—wrote that Linley "owes an unacknowledged debt" to my Fantasy Furniture exhibition and book.) The Viscount says *Extraordinary,* I say *Fantasy,* but unlike the Ira Gershwin song about trans-Atlantic miscommunication, I was not about to "call the whole thing off." In fact, the more I thought about it, the more I wanted to sue the copycat.

Catching wind of my criticisms, in late November 1996, Ruth Kennedy, the managing director of David Linley Furniture, Ltd., sent me a fax. With some tartly worded saber rattling, Kennedy attacked me for making "scurrilous charges" and "libelous comments about David and his book." By "accusing" Linley "of plagiarizing" *Fantasy Furniture,* she continued, I was taking a "very substantial risk of subjecting [myself] to damages." Adding further insults, Kennedy concluded her missive by writing that "we trust that you will cease defaming David Linley and stop spreading false and vicious rumors."

This was really too much. I'd been deliberately temperate in my comments about *Extraordinary,* and refrained from imputing any actionable motives to Linley. And besides, *I* was the wronged party here, not the Viscount. Aggravating me further, Kennedy admitted, deep in her fax, that despite his earlier denial, the Viscount and his research assistant *had* "generally looked at" *Fantasy.* But his decision to omit it from *Extraordinary*'s bibliography, "was made in good faith, based on objective standards, and not intended to be a slight of you or your book."

At the end of her correspondence, Kennedy said that she'd be in New York in December and asked if me and my lawyers wanted to meet her and hers. I took this as a sign that Linley was less than confident about his position and wanted to seek a peaceable solution. No way, I thought, shooting back to Ms. Kennedy a fax declining a sit-down. Then, goaded by my own irritation, I started ratcheting up the heat.

I contacted *New York* magazine and in early December, the magazine reported on my dust-up with the Viscount.

DAVID LINLEY GETS A NEW CREDIT LINE

read the headline, followed by my accusation that Linley "borrowed heavily from uncredited sources" in writing *Extraordinary Furniture,* which, to my gratification, the magazine described as "somewhat reminiscent" of *Fantasy Furniture.* Even better, the article quoted a "spokeswoman" from the Linley camp who conceded that my book "was left out of [*Extraordinary's*] bibliography. When the book is reprinted, that will be looked into." Not quite a full confession of culpability, but close. I felt I was getting somewhere.

A few days later, however, Linley retracted his almost confession.

CHIPPY LINLEY UP IN ARMS
FOR FURNITURE WARS

cried a headline in the London-based tabloid, *The Express.* The article went on to state that the "Queen's carpenter nephew has taken grave exception" to accusations that his book bore "uncanny similarities to another work." (Notice that everyone involved in, or writing about, our dispute avoided the "P" word.). "Linley is confident that he has done no wrong," *The Express* assured its readers.

That's not what Rizzoli thought, however. On December 6, publisher of Rizzoli International Publications Solveig Williams sent me a fax stating that "it seems indeed that the text of *Extraordinary Furniture* leans very heavily" on *Fantasy Furniture*—and although Linley's book "isn't a straight copy" of my book, I "should have at least gotten an acknowledgment for providing a primary source." I could ask for compensation from Linley, Williams continued, "but it will have to be [my] own decision." Rizzoli, it seemed, no longer had publication rights for *Fantasy* (those rights, in fact, had returned to me), and was not able to serve as my second in any duel with the Viscount.

So instead, I retained top-notch New York publicist Joanne Creveling. Within days, Joanne and I had drafted a press release repeating my criticism of *Extraordinary* while denying that I had made any "libelous" or "scurrilous" charges against the Queen's woodworking relative.

I was in high dudgeon. But a little voice kept asking me: what, exactly, was I doing? According to the press release, I was "considering my rights and options," i.e., still thinking about a lawsuit. To see the royal "borrower" in court—oh, the satisfaction that would bring! Not because of the money, of course. No, there was a principle involved here—the principle of being acknowledged for one's work. That's all I wanted. Well, no, maybe not all: Linley, I thought, needed a comeuppance. When I went to England in late 1996 and again in the spring of 1997, dealers aware of the imbroglio encouraged me to take legal action. The Viscount, it seemed, had stirred up resentment among London antiques dealers by opening his swank, reproduction-based business in the midst of the antiques shops of Pimlico Road. On a more personal level, the Linley camp began branding me in the press as "vicious" a "finger-pointer," and a "name-caller."

By the spring of 1997, I decided to force the issue. There was a piece in the gossipy "Page Six" section of the *New York Post* where I presented myself as "poised to sue" the Viscount. In a conciliatory gesture, however, I stated that I'd be satisfied if Linley apologized, acknowledged *Fantasy* in subsequent editions of *Extraordinary* and—since he called himself a "designer"—made an exculpatory donation to a leading school of design, Pratt Institute. This way, I thought, I could gain satisfaction without the bloodshed of a legal fight.

But Linley refused. He was, in a way, calling my bluff. Was it time to cry havoc and let slip the dogs of law?

No, advised my *consigliere*, Judy. She reminded me that several lawyers had described how expensive and difficult international plagiarism cases are to pursue. Moreover, she added, Linley had been stung enough by the turmoil: the American publications *New York Magazine* and the *New York Post,* as well as the English newspaper the *Daily Express* were calling him a "copycat" while suggesting that he may have "royally screwed-up" by not crediting my book. It was also possible that he didn't do all the research for *Extraordinary*—that some assistant had done it, and that he or she had "borrowed" from *Fantasy,* thinking that no one would notice. How much more embarrassment did I want Linley to suffer?

Besides, there was a larger issue here. By going against a member of the British royal family, I might look envious or resentful of his position and social standing. Even if I won a plagiarism suit—by no means a sure thing—I could end up being the loser in the court of public opinion. And that, Judy suggested, would darken the whole concept of Fantasy Furniture.

That point hit home. Sure, I knew that an international plagiarism suit would prove a major pain, uncertain, expensive, a huge time swallower, but the temptation to pursue it lingered. Especially since I still felt a sense of unsatisfied grievance but the thought that I might take the lightness, humor, and grace of Fantasy Furniture and plunge it into a grueling lawsuit—well, that was a vision too ironic and painful to bear. Fantasy Furniture was *my* contribution to the antiques field, my legacy. Did I want to involve it with lawyers, courts, legal briefs?

I remember a piece of advice I once heard about seeking revenge or retribution—"if it feels good, don't do it." Meaning that if by carrying out an action you would obtain a feeling of personal satisfaction, it's often best not to act. We should be wary of doing something just to "prove a point." In those situations, our motivations are usually more about pride than principle—and of all the spurs to action, pride is the most problematic. I wanted to sue Linley mostly because of injured self-respect, I realized—which was precisely why I shouldn't do it.

So I listened to Judy—and, as usually happens when I do, I was the better man for it. The matter faded from the press and, with no more breast thumping from either my side or Linley's, the issue was soon forgotten. Until now, of course.

And no, I'm not going to say I stopped feeling angry at the Viscount—pride is, after all, a difficult emotion to master. But I kept the joy and fantasy in Fantasy Furniture and my legacy free

from bitterness and rancor. A moral victory, I'd say—one that today gives me more satisfaction than any victory in a lawsuit.
Sometimes you really can win by turning another cheek.

As I said, it wasn't a huge issue. But it remained for years
something I wanted people to know the truth about. Now you
do. And notice, please, that the Viscount David Linley is listed in
the index of this book. Even if I'm still waiting for the day that
I'm acknowledged in the bibliography of *Extraordinary Furniture.*

Part Three

Tips and Tactics

Chapter Eleven

How and Where to Buy

Back when I was an active dealer, hardly a day passed when someone didn't approach me seeking information or advice about antiques. Not surprising, I guess, given the prominence of Newel in the field. Like any conscientious dealer, I was happy to share my knowledge and expertise: in the antiques business, it only helps to have a more educated public. (And by the way, I've just offered my first piece of advice: *always* ask questions of a dealer, no matter how uninformed you fear you might sound. If the dealer refuses to answer, or makes you feel foolish asking, leave—there's always another shop down the block.)

Over the years, I noticed that people generally asked me the same sorts of questions. The first had to do with my personal taste—how did I decorate my home? What antiques did I use? Others asked where and how did I buy Newel's inventory, what were my tactics, tricks, techniques? Lastly, collectors new to the field wanted advice on numerous topics, such as negotiating with European dealers, determining the actual worth of an antique, or dealing with those 800-pound gorillas, Christie's and Sotheby's.

If nothing else, these questions made me realize how little information is really out there. And that's a shame, for as I noted, the more people know about antiques and antiques dealers, the better for everyone. So in a spirit of disclosure and revelation, I thought I'd devote the following chapters of my memoirs to answering the most frequent questions posed to me, and hopefully dispel some of the mystery surrounding my profession. And who can resist the temptation to loosen the tie, put the feet up on the desk and expound on matters one has spent a lifetime pursuing?

So, what kind of antiques do I live with? I want to say every kind, for although it's not exactly true, when you consider that my apartment contains objects dating from the eighteenth to the twentieth centuries, it might as well be. Fortunately, Judy and I share a similar taste for soft colors and unusual furniture placed in unique combinations. And if you're thinking Brighton Pavilion, you're on the right track.

For instance, our living room includes an ninteenth-century English red lacquered secretary, black lacquered chairs and an eight-foot gilt palm tree enclosed by pale celadon walls; adding to the exotic, but comfortable, feeling of this room is a baby grand piano covered by a nineteenth-century embroidered table cover, upon which sits a selection of caricature candlesticks featuring mythological beings, enamel dragons, grinning devils, and other imaginative characters.

Or take our den: here we've assembled a number of Fantasy

pieces—a late nineteenth-century camel-shaped end table, a child's seat carved with miniature bears, a large horn and antler desk—along with two Biedermeier club chairs, a life-size bust of a Creole banjo player (the very piece that Michael Jackson declined to purchase) and paintings depicting dogs and hunting scenes set on walls covered with paisley fabric. Other highlights of our home include a white Art Deco bedroom with eggshell parchment veneered chest of drawers, a nineteenth-century Venetian console with blackamoor figures serving as legs in our dining room, as well as an eight-foot pre-Raphaelite painting, Italian Directoire chairs and two humorously contorted nineteenth-century carved wooden acrobats, about five feet tall, who greet guests entering our apartment foyer.

In fact, my idea was to create different environments in each room, each environment embodying that essence of movement, color and humor I find so attractive. It's like the visual equivalent of music—the flow, the intonations, the surprising counterpoint of melodies and tempos, from the *capriccio* of a Fantasy sideboard to the *adagio* of a Chippendale satinwood dining table, all blending into surprising harmony. If this sounds like something you might want to try in your own home, I have to warn you to be careful. In design, as in music, polyphony is tricky—different furniture periods and styles can clash against the eye like a Schoenberg sonata against the ear. To pull it off successfully, you need certain design elements to draw your objects together.

Chief among these elements—in my mind—is color. You can place fifteen pieces of all different characters and complexions in a single room, and with carefully chosen color unite them into a mutually cooperative ensemble. I've found that lighter colors seem the most accepting of eclectic furnishings, with a soft beige probably the most tolerant hue of all. Another important element is texture. Careful attention to the texture of objects can form visual "rhymes" that enhance any décor—in our case, the sheen of lacquered furniture chimes nicely against crisp Art Deco designs, while the slender carriage of bamboo furniture complements any type accessory.

This short, and hardly exhaustive, description of our home furnishings and design scheme begs another question I'm frequently asked: where did you buy your antiques?

This is a large topic, but I can tell you right away where I didn't buy my antiques: at auction. Not just because of my distaste for the auction process, but also because pieces that fall under the hammer are rarely "fresh"—that is, they've been on the market awhile. (No wonder, when you consider that at least sixty percent of furniture consignments to auctions come from dealers.)

So let's cut right to the chase. I went to Europe. A lot. At least 200 trips, logging in over two million miles. I'd go at all times of year, except July and August, when the Europeans take their interminable summer holidays. Not that I went everywhere on the Continent: Germany I always found disappointing—all that ponderous *lumpen* furniture—Mother Russia was generally destitute of good antiques, while the Eastern Bloc countries saw most of their fine objects disappear thanks to the war and the resulting Communist occupation. Every once and awhile I'd swing by the Scandinavian countries, or Belgium and Italy. But for serious antiques buying, there are really only two destinations worth expending time and resources: Paris and London. And cue Sinatra's "Come Fly With Me," because it's to those two cities we travel now.

Paris. The Eiffel Tower. Notre Dame. The Champs Elyseés and the Louvre. Street corner cafés, where you can watch the world go by as you nurse a demitasse of café. In all my trips to the City of Light, did I ever go to any of these places? Yes, but not often. My interest in Paris focused on the *marché aux puces,* or flea market, located in the northern suburb of Saint-Ouen. This was the largest flea market *du monde,* nearly 3,000 dealers packed into a roughly twelve-acre rabbit warren of booths, stands, alleyways and streets, selling every imaginable antique, from vintage bicycles to Louis XVI candelabra. Throw in crowds of people, car horns blaring, skulking pickpockets, ever-present piles of dog poop (the curse of Paris), and hundreds of international dealers all searching for choice antiques and you have the closest thing to Heaven I've ever experienced.

It's a confusing scene, to say the least—but here's how I handled it: I'd arrive in Paris on a Thursday night and head immediately to my hotel, a "deluxe boutique" hotel called Castille, located on the rue Cambon. Not only was the Castille ideally located, but it featured one of the best Italian restaurants in the city, Alain Ducasse's Il Cortile (and I love Italian food!) After a quick meal, I'd get to bed early, for by 6 A.M. Friday morning, I'd be in Saint Ouen, alert and primed for the hunt.

The flea market is open Saturdays to Mondays, Fridays they're closed to allow dealers time to set up their booths. For that reason, the *secret* is to go on a Friday to find fresh objects, before they're snatched up by buyers when the market opens the following day. So there I'd be, in the pre-dawn chill waiting for the telltale sound of a delivery truck backing into place, or an antiques booth's front shutter clattering up—whereupon I'd hustle to that place and, flashlight in hand, prowl through the dealer's inventory even as he was unpacking it. At first the dealers grumbled and complained about the intrusive American, but once they got to know me and realized that I was a serious buyer, they began to welcome my presence. Interestingly, in all my years of playing the early-bird antiques hunter, I rarely saw any of my compatriots snooping about at those hours. One exception was Parisian dealer Bernard Steinitz, who I'd sometimes see at dawn, flashlight similarly in hand. I guess that's why he is such a renowned figure in the business. He, too, had the drive, that inexplicable obsession to uncover rare and unseen artifacts.

After Saint Ouen, I directed my driver to take me to the Left Bank. By now it was early afternoon, lunch was a sandwich and Coke in the back of the car, the first thing I'd eat all day. I was so focused, so intent on scouring every antiques source I could. There are about 120 shops on the Rive Gauche—I had to visit them all. With obsessive anxiety, I went from door to door, driven by the thought that one shop I passed over might hold some undiscovered pearl I could bring to market. I never thought about getting tired and never stopped to socialize with the French dealers. For it never ceased, my father's voice, echoing in my thoughts, urging me on: *remember, don't come back until you find it.*

Finally, exhausted, I'd return to the Castille, have some dinner at Il Cortile, and go to bed.

At six on Saturday morning, it started all over again: Saint

Ouen by flashlight, keeping an eye out for whoever was opening their stand, poking through their antiques even before they drank their first café. Then, by early afternoon, when the market began filling up with camera-toting tourists, I was back at the Left Bank, combing through whatever stores I'd missed the previous day. (Shops on the Rive Gauche have infuriatingly irregular hours, so it's easy to arrive at an address only to find it closed.) My idea was to keep moving, keep searching, blitz the markets and purchase all the top-quality antiques I could find.

Now, out-hustling the competition was one thing; dealing with *les antiquaires français* was another. They can be an intimidating lot, these dealers, with their stony expressions, indifferent attitude, and unpronounceable language—but I found a way to beard the Gallic lion in its den. How? Well, to begin with, I never bargained in French—why hand the dealers even more of a home-court advantage? Instead, I equipped myself with a handful of French sentences—among them *je ne parle pas français* and *pouvez-vous baisser le prix?* I also carried a notepad and pencil, an integral part of my negotiating tactics. Whenever I saw an object I liked, I asked the dealer to write his price on the pad; then, glancing at the price, I'd exclaimed in a stagey voice, *"no, no, monsieur, c'est cra-zeee, cra-zeee!"* Scratching out his figure, I'd replace it with my own amount, usually fifty percent lower. He, in turn, would put on his act—shrugging, blowing out his lips, French-style—then he'd write a counter-offer on the pad, and in this way we'd do business. Not only did the pad compensate for my lack of French (and the Frenchman was certainly not going to speak English), it also helped diffuse tensions between us, as did the exaggerated humor I brought to the negotiations. *"Je suis un pauvre americain,"* I pleaded, and the dealers would laugh. Everyone knew there was no such thing as a poor American.

Once I bought a piece, I paid right away, and made sure the dealer knew that my shipper—Alan Franklin, a Paris-based Englishman with whom I worked for years—would send people by within the hour to pick up the object. I didn't want my antiques sitting around with my purchase tags exposed on them, letting other dealers know what I'd bought. More importantly, Parisian dealers are not above removing tags. For example, at the *marché Serpette* in Saint-Ouen, I once discovered a pair of Louis XVI benches, one in good condition, the other considerably worse. I bought the first bench, only to find when my shipment arrived in New York, that I'd been sent the second, less desirable, bench. It had been no mistake. Clearly, the dealer had received a better offer for the first bench and switched my tag so that Alan innocently picked up the wrong object. A small peccadillo, perhaps—but a word to wise, nonetheless.

In any case, on Sundays I'd check out of the Castille early in the morning, make one last check of the flea market, then head to de Gaulle Airport for a flight across the Channel. In truth, though, I'd already started my work in England. London shops are closed on Sundays, so while still in Paris I'd telephone and make appointments with dealers located in the countryside. I'd land at Heathrow, meet my driver and immediately set off in one of three directions leading from London—west to Bath, north to the Cotswolds, or south to Brighton. Along these routes (which I'd alternate each time I returned to England) lay many of the best dealers in the UK, especially for unique, exotic, and otherwise high-quality objects. I'd do my purchasing, then turn around and head back to London, winding up Sunday night at the Four Seasons, where I frequently stayed.

Buying antiques in Britain is 180 degrees opposite to buying on the Continent. For one thing, as opposed to the early morning hurly-burly of the *marché aux puce,* antique hunts on the Sceptered Isle are leisurely affairs. The shops usually don't open until 10 A.M., so you have plenty of time to enjoy a good breakfast and read a newspaper. And rather than Gaulois-puffing, vaguely contemptuous Parisians, English dealers are relaxed and welcoming, and usually insist on making you a spot of tea (a good sign that they mean to do business). The British generally like Americans and lack the Frenchman's annoying chip on the *épaule.* By the same token, however, you have to treat our Anglo cousins more carefully. You can huff and puff and roar at French dealers and they generally won't mind: all they want to do is sell you antiques. But for the English, it's still a genteel business, and you have to be correspondingly more discrete and sensitive: abruptness—a key element when dealing with the French— comes off in England as deal-killing rudeness. And when a Brit offers you his initial price, you should try to reduce it by twenty-five percent, rather than half.

This situation was the same in London, where I would work on Monday and Tuesday. Up and down fashionable Pimlico Road, Kings Road (where there are some of the best sources in London), Camden Passage (which has hundreds of small shops but only operates Tuesday to Saturday), Fulham Road (for quality furniture), Kensington Church Street (a good source for eclectic items), and finally Westbourne Grove and Portobello Road (which is fun to visit on Saturday). While I toured these areas I'd play the perfect gentleman, charming the Brits and being charmed in return, playing to their eagerness to sell, even as they played to mine to buy. Once, however, I fear my Yankee instincts slipped the leash. It was a Sunday evening. I was motoring down Fulham Road in London en route to the Four Seasons after a day in the countryside, when I saw a truck backed against an empty store and workers unloading what looked to be antiques. I took note of the address, and first thing Monday morning, I had my driver return me there. The store, no longer empty, now bore a large sign reading HEMISPHERE ANTIQUES. Although it hadn't yet opened for business, I tapped on the window. The owner came out from the back, and I was surprised to see that he was a young American dealer I knew named Raymond Painter. Raymond recognized me, as well, and seemed strangely nervous as he opened the door. I soon discovered why. His store was filled with spectacular French Art Deco objects—material you normally didn't see in London.

After looking around for a few minutes, I told Raymond there were a number of pieces that I liked.

He swallowed. "Which ones?" he asked.

"All of them."

This is what the young man feared. "Bruce, you can't," he demurred. "you'll leave me with nothing!"

"Come on, Raymond," I insisted.

"Bruce, please, I haven't even opened for business yet!"

But I already had the checkbook out. "Raymond, look," I reasoned. "Why sit around and wait for these pieces to be sold one by one? I'm willing to take them off your hands all at once.

You can go on vacation now without ever having been open a day."

It was, as they say, an offer he couldn't refuse. He sold me the entire inventory of his store in one quick shot. Thirty superb Art Deco furnishings and accessories that looked even better once I displayed them at Newel.

You're probably thinking, that's all very interesting, but I like to hunt for antiques, too—what are my chances of having your success in Europe?

Well, therein lies the rub. Unless you're an experienced dealer with a checkbook as deep as a well, the chances aren't great—not at first, at least. Not because you're not a savvy negotiator or heads-up connoisseur about antiques, but—well, as the old adage goes, you've got to pay your dues. Things take time. After you make a few trips to Europe and become familiar with the dealers in Paris and London, you'll be surprised how accommodating they will be about leading you to other sources where you can find top items. More importantly, you'll soon learn which dealers have the best material for periods that interest you, thereby reducing your search time. Even better, you'll discover in both cities which dealers—and there are always a handful of them—have warehouses within walking distance of their shops. Eventually, you can persuade one or two to take a break from hanging about the cafés or pubs and gossiping about politics to lead you through their hidden caches. It's the equivalent of a merchant putting a finger to his lips, pulling the shade down over his stand and leading you into a back room where he keeps his real merchandise. It took me time to learn this, and I bought some of my best antiques this way.

Still, there are short cuts to learning your way around Paris and London. Several Parisian and British packing and shipping companies offer drivers (known as couriers) who will take you to "choice" antique sources. But beware: dealers often pay these drivers to take tourists to their shops; as soon as they see you get out of the car, they identify you as a "rube," and jack up their prices. On the other hand, most of these drivers are honest and really do know the markets and sources to buy good antiques— just keep in mind their sometimes unscrupulous practices and re- member, always, *caveat emptor.* (And don't forget your notepad and pencil!)

I should also remark upon one other problematic aspect about buying in Europe. I don't know how many times I over- heard French and British dealers making fun of American tourists—and bragging about how they took some poor guy from Peoria for all they could get. For this reason, I caution you against hunting for antiques dressed in Yankee tourist couture— you know, sweatpants, T-shirts, fanny packs, and cameras strung around the neck like ID cards. (And if—God forbid—you wear a baseball hat backwards, you deserve the skinning you're liable to get from the Euro dealers!)

And for this reason, too, I do not suggest that you wander through West Sussex or the *marché Paul Bert* with your interior decorator in tow. You might as well hang two signs around your neck, next to your Nikon camera: I AM A WEALTHY TOURIST and I AM PREPARED TO BUY (for why else would you bring your deco- rator?) Don't be surprised if the price tags start putting on francs and pounds.

A couple of last points to keep in mind when shopping in Europe: once you've scrawled your John Hancock on the traveler's check, you're still not through paying for your antique. Practically every piece of furniture you purchase will require some sort of restoration work: refinishing or reupholstering, for example, or repairs to shaky legs, broken hinges, missing handles, that sort of thing—not to mention the high costs to transport and ship the objects to the States. So be prepared.

So let's see: snooty dealers, contempt for tourists, questionable business practices, language barriers, transportation and shipping costs—not to mention the normal risks in purchasing any antiques—why should anyone buy in Europe?

Because it's fun, exciting, educational—and there's something about warm beer in a English pub on a rainy afternoon in the Cotswolds that can't be beat. (The same could be said for a baguette, cheese, and a good bottle of wine in a Parisian café.) But there are more practical reasons: you're more likely to find outstanding objects at better prices across the pond than stateside. Foreign dealers are generally more active than their American counterparts: they spend more time in the countryside scouring for interesting objects, and seem more willing to sell them. Not to mention the fact that Europe is, well, old, and just naturally full of antiques.

In the U.S., by contrast, it seems that nearly every good antiques source from Maine to California has already been listed in one magazine or another. Worse, because of the success of TV programs like *Antiques Roadshow*, thousands of scavenger hunters are out there, scooping up anything and everything in hopes of finding some undiscovered marvel they can then flip on eBay. You can still unearth these pieces, of course, but you've got to look especially hard.

But in any case, why bother? Call me unpatriotic, but I think America has produced few great furniture designers—Duncan Phyfe, Goddard-Townsend, the Herters, Belter, Wright, perhaps one or two more, but that's about it. Much American furniture is just boring. You just don't have the decorative styles you find in Europe. Moreover, since the number of great pieces available is so small, prices tend to be much higher for American furniture than for European.

But furniture is furniture, and let's say while vacationing in the Great Smoky Mountains, you actually do find an American sideboard or chest of drawers that knocks you out. You want it—you've got that gotta have it feeling—and your hand starts reaching for your credit card. But wait! How do you know that the antique is worth the price? How do you know it's really an antique, really authentic—and how much restoration work does it need? How do you know you're not that poor guy from Peoria about to be taken for a ride? Important questions—and in the next chapter, I'll give you some answers for them.

Chapter Twelve

Is It Real or Repro?

It happened all the time. People new to the antiques field would express surprise at Newel's relatively high prices. "Why are your antiques so expensive?" they'd ask me, in tones ranging from surprise to indignation. My reply was always the same. "Because," I'd say, "I never want Newel to be known as cheap."

My answer may have been a bit facetious, but it contained several levels of meaning. Newel's prices were sometimes higher than other shops because we offered so many one-of-a-kind antiques, never before seen on the American market. Not only that, but—as you know from the previous chapter—I went to extraordinary lengths to find these items. Few people had any idea of what I—or other major dealers, for that matter—went through to build up inventory: the frustration, time and effort, shipping and refinishing expenses. Add in the normal costs of doing business, including wages, telephone, electric, rent, business and trade permits, fine arts and liability insurance, workman's compensation, medical group insurance, service contracts for elevators, security and sprinkler systems, federal, state, and city taxes plus a host of hidden taxes such a real estate occupancy tax and vault tax, in addition to a sliver of profit for the dealer—well, naturally prices are going to climb.

Bottom line: in antiques, as in life, excellence does not come cheap.

But my response was also an attempt to address the larger issue behind the question about Newel's prices. Then, as now, people were confused about the antique market, and how dealers set the value of the objects they sell. They wanted my assurance that I was charging them a proper amount and was not taking advantage of their naiveté. It's a perennial worry of almost every person once he or she begins putting serious money down on furniture and accessories: How do we know that we're paying a fair price when we buy an antique?

Well, how do you know?

If you're a private individual, you probably don't. That's just the fact of the matter. The bottom line is, you must have confidence with the dealer that you are visiting.

The majority of my colleagues are honest, hard-working professionals who'd rather strip the patina off a Queen Anne highboy than unethically jack up the price. But don't take my word for it. There are numerous ways to check the reputation of any dealer with whom you plan to do business. Word of mouth of friends is perhaps the best and easiest method. Ask around. Better yet, what's the opinion of interior decorators who work with nearly everyone in the trade? Run a Lexis-Nexus or Google search: is your dealer mentioned in the press (and not just the art press)? You can also check with several antiques trade organizations dedicated to maintaining professionalism among their members: the best of these organizations include the Art and Antique Dealers League of America, the Brussels-based Confederation Internationale des Negociants en Ouevres D'Art (CINOA), and the British Antique Dealers' Association, headquartered in London.

I must note that Newel does not belong to any of these groups. Because my father established our rock-solid reputation a generation ago, I never felt the need to join one. Besides, as I've said, part of my business strategy was to position Newel outside the normal fraternity of dealers.

Still, if reputation were everything, no one would need a doctor's second opinion. When it comes to antiques, if you're about to drop five figures on an Art Deco commode, it never hurts to first show the piece to another expert for his or her appraisal. Trust, but verify, as Ronald Reagan was fond of saying. Along these lines, it's also not a bad idea to do your own antiques research: read books, question dealers, peruse catalogues, attend auctions. One thing I don't suggest you do, however, is rely on those antique "price guides" found everywhere these days. These guides base their pricing information on auction records, which can give a skewed and incomplete view of the market. Rather than make you an instant expert, they're just as likely to leave you more confused than ever.

If you're a dealer, questions about price and value are much simpler. You really only have two points to consider. Does the piece have style and quality? And, can I sell it for more than I paid for it? Personally, I never worried about overpaying for an antique. Sometimes I had to take a smaller profit on a particular piece, but at least my competition didn't have it. Besides, you'll never go broke taking a small profit.

In the end, though, some antiques are so unusual or unique—the Edward VII lovechair, for example—that it's hard, if not impossible, for anyone to pinpoint their "true" value. The beauty of these objects, and the pleasure they give you, that's where their value lies. And, in turn, this means that the fair market price of an antique is often no more complicated than what someone is willing to pay for it. And not only antiques: I remember once when my friend John Marion auctioned off an Impressionist painting at Sotheby's for tens of millions of dollars and someone asked him if the painting was worth that much. "It is now," he replied. The bottom line here? If you love an antique, don't concern yourself with overpaying for quality. Over time, the piece will pay back your costs—and more.

Still, I'd frequently encounter the would-be antiques connoisseur who was convinced that I wanted to overcharge him (or, more rarely, her). No matter how patiently I'd explain that it's not in the interest of any reputable dealer to cheat the public, he was adamant—he knew the value of some object, and wasn't going to meet my price. If I were irritated enough by this know-it-all attitude, I'd use a psychological ploy perfected by Joseph Duveen. When one of his wealthy clients balked at paying a hefty sum for, say a Rembrandt or Reubens, the Baron would nod in acknowledgment, then say, "Yes, I see, perhaps you're not ready for this yet—" The insinuation being, of course, that the buyer's hesitation to pay for the masterpiece revealed his unsophistication—an imputation that usually induced the plutocrat to open his purse. As we know, Duveen was mostly right about the value of art—and when I used that tactic on hesitant antique buyers (usually with success), I was right, too.

So far, we've used examples where one is buying antiques from a reputable dealer on, say, Madison Avenue or King's Road. But let's say you're not in New York or London. Let's imagine you're in some rural area and you discover what could be the perfect piece for your apartment. Now the situation is trickier. The seller may claim it's from the eighteeenth century, but how do you know? How can you tell if the object has been restored, or is in fact a reproduction—or worse, a reproduction that someone has deliberately doctored to make it look old? (Complicating matters, the seller himself may have faulty or incomplete knowledge about the piece.) Nothing can substitute for an eye trained by years of antiques experience, of course. But I can alert you to basic clues about an object's authenticity—clues that may determine whether you'll become the possessor of a true antique treasure, or the owner of what the auction houses charmingly call an NSV (No Sale Value), a reproduction.

Let's start with a simple point: uniformity of wood. In the past, cabinetmakers often fashioned the exteriors of furniture using primary woods—such as mahogany, satinwood, walnut—while reserving for the interiors such secondary varieties as pine and oak. Today, on the contrary, many cabinetmakers generally rely on one type of wood for the entire object. This is particularly true in Asia, where manufacturers often use wood that resembles mahogany, but is of poorer quality. With this in mind, before you lay out money for that beautiful sideboard or cabinet, check its back, in addition to its drawers: if you find that these areas consist of a different, seemingly cheaper wood, smile. Secondary is good; secondary can mean antique; if these areas are of one wood, it's probably a repro.

If your prospective purchase is an armchair, flip it over. Most armchairs possess a piece of muslin or canvas stretched across the bottom to cover the springs. Pull back a corner and look for tack marks. A real antique, or at least an old piece, should have hundreds of marks from people who, over the years, have removed the covering to reupholster the chair or tighten the springs, then tacked it back into place. Many tack marks: possibly antique; smooth wood, probably reproduction.

"Contact points," or places where people regularly touched the object, are also crucial in determining whether an object has age or not. For example, let's say you're interested in a set of dining room chairs. If the chairs are true antiques, and not reproductions, the back rails should display worn spots where countless hands have gripped the chairs to move them. Skin oil is the Carbon-14 of antiques: over the years, it soaks into furniture, building up in areas like the tops of chair arms, where it wears away gilt, darkens wood and leaves other telltale indications that an object is old. Forgers—or people who try various tricks to make reproductions look antique—will mimic these signs, but they rarely, if ever, capture the subtle effects of time and human physicality on furniture.

Another place to look for evidence of age is low down on chair and table legs. Do the "ankles" bear nicks and "bruises" caused by blows from careless feet, wayward mops, and overly ag-

gressive vacuum cleaners? Do chair bottoms show uneven surfaces resulting from years—if not centuries—of people moving
them back and forth in order to the clean the floors? And how
about the splats—the braces beneath a chair's seat that reinforce
the legs? They, too, should exhibit signs of countless shoes striking
their surfaces. Here again, forgers attempt to "age" reproduction
legs by deliberately banging up their ankles, bottoms and splats,
but they tend to make the furniture look too distressed, or leave
marks in patterns too orderly to be random.

Another characteristic of antiques difficult for forgers to duplicate are wormholes. As we know, these creatures' larvae nestle
in furniture wood, and after hatching, chew their way to the surface, creating tiny little tunnels. Obviously, anyone with a fine
enough drill bit can recreate this effect. What *you* need to do is
stick a needle in the hole: if the course of the tunnel is irregular,
chances are its creator was nature; if the needle goes straight in,
figure Black & Decker.

Anyway, you get the idea. There is not a single antique in
existence that is not old. And if it is truly old, it will almost always
bear the marks of its interactions with the world. People attempt
to reproduce scuffs and bruises and oil patches on newer pieces,
but nine times out of ten, you can detect the deception.

In any case, though, out-and-out fakes—or reproductions
that a seller knowingly and deceitfully sells as antique—aren't the
real problem. No, what causes beginners and experts alike the
most trouble are pieces of furniture that are only partially original, that contain elements from other, usually newer, sources. To
put it another way, an eighteenth-century Hepplewhite dining
table with twenty-first-century reproduction Hepplewhite legs

(you can buy them online!) is probably not the antique you thought you bought in that New England tent sale. How can you tell if an antique is truly authentic, or is in fact a hybrid—or "marriage"—of different pieces? What are the signs that an antique has undergone alteration or restoration at some time in its existence—and does that always matter?

A major clue to the authenticity of an antique is the patina, style, and grain of the wood. In the same way that a checkered shirt worn with a pin-stripe suit suggests something possibly wrong about the wearer, a table leg and top with mismatched grains and different tones of wood may indicate that your piece is not a true antique.

Remember what I said about the different woods often used by furniture manufacturers in the past? Here's something else to look for: over the years, what with the swelling and shrinkage caused by changes in temperature and humidity, the less durable wood used for rear panels often cracks. So pull that highboy from the wall—in many instances, not only will the back wood appear less attractive, but it may be cracked. And that's good; that shows age.

And don't forget the drawers. These are particularly important because a piece that is otherwise antique may contain one or more reproduction drawers replacing those that were lost over time. Now, I've already mentioned that the exteriors of antique drawers often exhibit better quality wood than the interiors. But you should also examine a drawer's "dovetails," or the crenellated wooden teeth that hold the sides together with the front. If the drawer in question dates from before the era of machine-made furniture, the dovetails were cut by hand—and as such, should be irregularly sized and spaced. If they're as regular as chiclets, you've probably got a repro. Lastly, it's not a bad idea to rub the underside of a drawer—if it was hand-made, it will undoubtedly exhibit a rough and uneven surface. And we know what rough and uneven can mean: antique.

But that's not all you can learn from the humble drawer. Take the keyhole, which is usually surrounded by a small metal plate, or an "escutcheon." Years of repeated polishing should create a residue of brass and furniture polish around the edges and in the etching of the escutcheon—a sign of age that's difficult to duplicate. By the same token, it's quite simple to pull out the tiny nails—or "brads"—that hold an escutcheon to the piece and examine the underlying wood. The holes should line up in a way that suggests that the escutcheon originally belonged to the drawer. And take notice of the underlying wood: if it's an antique, the wood should appear lighter, since the air and years of polishing did not get to it.

Obviously, when you buy an antique from a dealer you should ask for an invoice that lists a full description of the object: its age, provenance, and other pertinent details, including whether the dealer believes that the piece bears any restoration work. And remember, the more restorations, the lower the object's value. But does this mean you should reject an antique if it has any restoration work? Here's where your own taste comes in. A seventeenth-century table fitted with legs made in the eighteenth is still an antique, whereas the same table with legs fashioned last week in Malaysia is a poor marriage and probably a reproduction. Then, too, if you find a beautiful early Georgian dressing table that contains a single drawer with even dovetails—well, maybe that's one imperfection you can live with. Again, these decisions are up to you. My only concern is that you possess as much information as possible about your purchase. As I've said before in this book, and many times in my career, the more knowledgeable people are about antiques, the better it is for the trade and the public alike.

Individual taste plays an important role in another, more controversial, area of antiques: patina. Patina, of course, is the accumulation of marks, discolorations, wine stains, cigarette burns and other evidence of time and human interaction that naturally accrue to the surface of an antique, and which can add to the object's appeal. No two people, however, agree on how much or what kind of patina an antique should possess. Some people like their antiques to look as old and dignified as the iconic faces of Georgia O'Keefe or Samuel Beckett. Others, especially those who prefer ormolu-laden *meubles francaises,* like their antiques as bright and shiny as Britney Spears' navel ring.

My personal feeling about patina is that a little bit goes a long way. Today, many antique buyers make a fetish of age markings, snapping up furniture that looks like it served as the backboard for a Chicago Bulls game. Just because time has beaten a piece into submission doesn't make it beautiful. On the other hand, others go to the opposite extreme and strip off the patina, attempting to make their antiques as fresh as the day they were made. My advice is to give your furniture a polishing every couple of years. That way, you don't destroy the patina, but neither do you abandon your pieces to the depredations of time and human behavior.

Another point to consider when caring for antiques is the

fact that, like you and me, furniture breathes. Air circulates around each piece, having a pronounced impact over the years, especially in dry climates, where a lack of humidity can cause cracks to appear in antique wood and veneers to bubble. To prevent these effects, you can purchase a humidifier—it's good for your health and your antiques—and keep to an every-couple-years' polishing regime. But be careful about the type of polish you use—for example, avoid linseed oil, which, because of its viscosity and stickiness, tends to attract dust and dirt.

Obviously, an antique so damaged that it is unattractive or non-functional is probably not much use to anybody. But what about perfectly fine pieces that have fallen out of fashion—what can we do with these? Adapt, modify, and improvise. For example, because of the prevalence of closets these days, the original purpose of armoires is pretty much obsolete. But apply a little adaptive carpentry work and you've got a fine "tech tower" to hold your home entertainment system. Or take a washstand: I've seen many of these objects refitted to make attractive bathroom sinks. Headboards, too: in the past, beds were smaller. To accommodate today's larger king-size beds, why not take two headboards and fit them together to make a single great piece? Or put a pair of beautiful gates together to fashion an interesting headboard? With imagination, your options can be limitless.

My favorite improvisation is the coffee table. Every once in awhile, the host of some dinner party will proudly exhibit to me his "antique coffee table." I don't have the heart to inform him that such an object is an oxymoron—coffee tables are purely a modern invention. Instead, interior decorators often take an antique bench, remove the upholstery and slap a plank of wood or a piece of marble on top to form an "old" table. Sometimes this gets a little humorous. I remember years ago a decorator who would regularly come by Newel with his latest client. He'd spend a few minutes wandering about the shop, before asking me to take him to our benches. "Hmmm, these are nice," he'd muse, pulling on his chin. Then, as if struck by an inspiration, he'd exclaim, "Hey, Bruce, you know what? We could replace the top of this bench and turn it into an antique coffee table! Isn't that a fabulous idea?" The first time I believed his act; by the tenth repetition, I realized it was shtick intended to impress his client and began escorting the decorator to our bench section before he'd even ask.

My point is, antiques are part of our decorative arts family. We want them around as long as possible. And if transforming an otherwise obsolete piece into modern usage changes its original appearance, so what? If the choice is between the junk heap or new life as a restored and modernized object of beauty, which do you think is better?

Having said all this, I want to close this chapter on a cautionary note. Nothing I've written here should imply a formula for determining the age or authenticity of a particular antique. There's no such thing. Even with years of training and experience it's not always easy to tell the real from the fake. Even the best eye in this business can be fooled—especially if the forger is a brilliant artist in his own right. And if you think I'm building to an anecdote about how I was almost tricked—well, read on.

The incident took place in Paris. While scouring the flea market one morning, I came upon some bronze wall sconces displayed in an outdoor stand. Interested, I examined them, concluding they were probably eighteenth century.

"These pieces are very attractive," I remarked to the dealer, pulling out my notebook and pencil. But a nagging doubt caused me to hold off on the negotiations, and instead ask, "Can you give me more information about them?"

The dealer shrugged, stubbed out a cigarette butt with his shoe, then replied, "I think you must ask Jacques about the sconces. It is Jacques who makes them."

At first I thought I misunderstood. Jacques makes the sconces? But the metal, the screws, the patina, they looked so authentic—I was shocked and intrigued. Knowing the skill of my eye, I figured that whoever this Jacques was, he must be a *very* talented craftsman. I had to meet him. I obtained his address from the dealer, and set off in search of the mystery artisan.

Before long, I found myself on a small cobblestone street just outside St. Ouen. I knocked on the door of a nondescript building and a young man answered. After a few minutes of conversation, he took me up a small staircase. As I approached the top landing, I heard the unmistakable tap-tap-tap of light hammers striking metal. Inside a tiny room were four men, one of whom, an elderly gentlemen, introduced himself as Jacques.

"My work pleases you, monsieur?" he asked.

"It *astonishes* me," I replied. All the more so as I realized that in this veritable cubbyhole, Jacques and his workmen fashioned objects from scratch that appeared two centuries old. They distressed the metal just enough—no exaggerated scuffs marks here—and created by hand eighteenth-century style screws and fasteners that would have fooled a museum curator. More amazing yet, these weren't fakes, but entirely original designs. It was as if a group of twentieth-century painters, imbued with the genius of the Rembrandt School, were creating artworks that seemed to originate from seventeenth-century Amsterdam.

"Aren't you concerned about the ethics of what you're doing?" I asked Jacques. "If a professional antiques dealer like me can believe your work is authentic, what about other potential buyers, not as knowledgeable as me?"

Jacques gave the traditional French shrug and puff of the lips. "*Qu'est-ce que je peux dire, monsieur?* It is always a matter of caution. Or, as the saying goes, *caveat emptor,* oui?"

Oui. And that, of course, is one of the points of this anecdote. You can trust, you can verify, but in the end, you've got to be careful, because antiques will always surprise you. It's this element of surprise that makes them so alluring, of course. Surprise—and beauty. And that's the second point of this story: it's the beauty of antiques, the aesthetic pleasure they give us, that's most important, not their physical condition or level of authenticity. In other words, if you love something—buy it, chances are you won't regret your decision. I know. As I write this, I'm looking at a fantastic bronze doré end table I once bought in Paris. It looks for all the world like it was made in the eighteenth century—but, in fact, if anybody asks, I reveal that it was made by a master craftsman just a few years ago. I love this table. For although it may not be a true antique—it is certainly a masterpiece.

Chapter Thirteen

Clean Up the Act

I introduced this book with an anecdote about Jackie Kennedy—not only because it's a fond memory, but also because her example of style and taste did much to glamorize my chosen profession, antiques. She wasn't alone, of course. There was Hollywood, and the lavish movie sets, which first introduced mass audiences to beautiful interiors. And Peter Wilson, whose marketing genius transformed auctions into glamorous social affairs. Nor should we overlook a celebrity collector like Barbra Streisand, and how she helped make antiques fashionable. Even Newel, with its encyclopedic inventory and revolutionary advertising, played a role in expanding the public's idea of the antiques trade.

The point is, the antiques business has been growing rapidly. From a small guild dominated by a few specialists in English and

French furniture, the field has blossomed into a billion dollar industry that supports countless galleries, interior designers, auction
houses, and publications. With this growth, the image of the antiques dealer has changed, as well: instead of the proverbial snob
affecting European mannerisms and tastes, today's dealers consist
of every conceivable type of person—from tweedy academics to
"buy-'n'-flip" specialists who work eBay like modern-day pros-
pectors panning for gold.

So far, I've stressed the positive aspects of the modern antiques boom. Now, however, I want to add some notes of caution. In some ways, my beloved avocation has grown too much,
too fast over the years. Don't get me wrong. I'm thrilled that
more people are earning a living buying and selling antiques. It's
just that in many subtle, and not-so-subtle, ways I feel that the
level of connoisseurship, expertise and professionalism has declined. This troubles me. I've stressed many times that you should
carefully check the authenticity of the antiques you buy—well,
the same holds true for the dealers and the designers who help
you buy them. There are some bad apples out there. How can
you tell who's legit and who's not? Let me give you some tips—
along with other observations about today's antiques industry.

Let's start with interior designers. Just about everyone uses
one these days—at least seventy percent of Newel's business was
done via designers. In many ways, they fueled today's booming
market. From Billy Baldwin helping Jackie remodel the White
House to Mario Buatta introducing another Upper East Side so-
ciety matron to the glories of chintz, these friends of the busy, the
taste-challenged and the ladies-who-lunch have helped spread

the gospel of antiques to the American public. Newel owes much of its success to them.

Now, most designers are smart, honest, occasionally brilliant individuals who can rescue you from do-it-yourself decorating errors and can actually save you money. By the same token, however, there are others who are best avoided like plastic sofa covers. Remember my story about the designer whose "inspiration" was to convert an antique bench into a coffee table? Unfortunately, he's not uncommon. Too many of them have a limited number of ideas that they apply in every situation—while making it seem as if they're spontaneously reacting to the needs of their clients. To give another example: a designer frequently brought clients into Newel, carrying with him armfuls of fabric and paint samples. He and his clients would so excitedly discuss antiques and colors and design schemes, you'd swear he was ablaze with creative thoughts and visions. Until, that is, after the third or fourth time of this routine, when you noticed that no matter the client, the designer always chose the same fabric and color samples.

You should watch out for designers with the Big Idea, or those who seem overly insistent on a particular design plan— chances are, that plan is all they've got: I call it "formula decorating." Beware, too, of designers inordinately fond of trends—today's shelter magazine photo spread can quickly become yesterday's stale idea. Lastly, think twice about the designer who wants to make a "statement" with your living quarters. It's possible his or her ideas will work and you'll become the envy of your friends and neighbors. But it's also possible you'll find yourself living in an extension of the designer's personality, not your own.

Bottom line: the ultimate decision on interior décor should fall to you, and should reflect your personality, not your designer's.

Even if you find a designer you're comfortable with, there's another pitfall to avoid: discounts. These are reductions on the price of antiques—usually around twenty percent—that dealers traditionally offer to designers. Personally, I dislike discounts and think the trade should abolish them. What's wrong with saving money? Unfortunately, it's never that simple: in fact, discounts frequently lead to more trouble than they're worth. Let me explain why.

Several years ago, a designer purchased a set of chairs from Newel for $30,000. According to a policy my father had established, we gave the designer a twenty percent discount—which meant that the designer actually paid $24,000 for the objects. Twelve years later, the client called us and said that she was redecorating her home and asked if we could take the chairs back. As I've mentioned, we were always happy to reclaim antiques. "Sure," I told her, "for $24,000 in store credit."

"Our bill says the chairs cost $30,000," the lady protested.

"I'm sorry," I replied, "but Newel charged your designer $24,000." I felt badly that the designer had not informed his client about the discount that we gave to him.

"Oh God," the woman gasped. "Wait until I tell my husband."

And wait until they tell the world about how the designer took advantage of them, I thought.

Discounts may seem like a good idea, but they frequently result in deceit, false expectations and bad feelings.

Often a designer's client would come into Newel alone, select an antique, and expect us to offer the same "courtesy" we extended to his or her designer. I'd then have to patiently explain
that discounts were available only for the trade. You can imagine
how well that went over with some of the Type-A-personality
bankers and lawyers who shopped at Newel!

Even worse, certain designers, seeking to disguise the fact
that they'd received a discount—or simply to overcharge their
clients—would sometimes ask us to do the unthinkable: change
the price tag. I recall an incident in the late '50s when a then-fa-
mous designer came into Newel and announced that her "very
important client" was coming in to look at a particular French
recamier which the designer had seen the day before. "Could you
make a new tag showing a higher price for the piece? she asked.
Then, to our astonishment, she added, "Could you also dirty the
tag up a little so my client thinks it's been attached to the recamier for awhile?" My father refused. And never did business
with the designer again.

This is why I have long advocated that people should draw
up contractual agreements clearly stating a set percentage that
they will pay designers above the purchase cost of antiques, carpets, fabrics and other decorating necessities. This is a more appropriate method of compensating designers for their time, expertise and talent. The old method must change and this more
transparent manner of doing business has got to become standard
in the trade. I feel strongly that discounts must be done away
with throughout the entire decorating industry.

So far, I've brought up negative images of designers—worst-
case scenarios, as it were. But to really understand the field, you

need a positive image, as well. An image of a great designer, someone with all the ingredients: taste, intelligence, and ethics. Someone who embodied the best of the profession and can act as a model from which you can judge the rest. Or to put it another way, you need to know about the late Mark Hampton.

Mark was justly famous, the designer other designers looked to, the epitome of a kind of patrician tolerance and grace. He was decisive, too—no hemming and hawing about antique purchases with him. And he could impart this decisiveness to his clients. Many's the time I saw him leap onto a chair or recamier, kick off his shoes and stretch out as if watching TV at home while smiling at his client as if to say, "See? This piece is perfect for your den!"

The press dubbed Mark the "First Decorator," referring to the fact that he helped design the White House for the first George Bush. His other clients included Jackie Onassis, Henry Kissinger, Mike Wallace, Estée Lauder, and Saul Steinberg. But more than just decorating their homes, Mark, with Duveen-like canniness and flair, knew how to lead his clients beyond their self-imposed limits. One day, for example, he came into Newel with dress designer Carolyn Rhoem, the second wife of Henry Kravis. Henry, it seemed, had purchased a ranch out west and the Kravis' wanted Mark to decorate it. Mark, however, had no intention of crafting a predictable "Western look"—you know, stools and rough-hewn hickory chairs, rawhide lampshades, and Navaho rugs—but instead, escorted Carolyn to the seventeenth-century Dutch and Spanish furniture. She loved the material and with a bit of subtle encouragement from Mark agreed that it would be perfect for her Western get-away. "But there's a problem," she demurred, "Henry. He likes everything pristine."

"Well," Mark sniffed, as if affronted by the idea of a mere billionaire challenging his design taste, "I'm certainly not going to give him a history lesson." A little cowed, I think, by Mark's sublime confidence, Carolyn wound up agreeing with him.

Even the small details about him were exquisite: he had, for example, the most gorgeous handwriting. He painted hundreds of watercolors and gave them as gifts to his family and friends. Raised in Indiana as a Quaker, he never lost that Midwestern spirituality, broad and deep, prizing friendship above nearly everything. He was generosity personified.

I was honored to call Mark a friend. He particularly liked Newel and regularly dropped by to purchase antiques and sometimes simply to chat. As I mentioned, he'd confide his embarrassment at the way that some women clients seemed to retain him simply so that they could be seen shopping around town with him. But that was Mark. A social cachet. A man whose company made others feel better about themselves.

His death from cancer in 1998 left a hole in many people's hearts—and in the decorative arts community, as well. He was irreplaceable. There are, however, a few young designers who I believe stand a good chance of at least partially filling his shoes. Among them, the South African-born New Yorker, Geoffrey Bradfield and Palm Beach's Scott Snyder. There are other very fine designers, of course, but these are among the leading lights of today's field.

Turning now from designers to dealers, we see a similar situation: explosive growth, expanding markets, changes both superficial and profound. As a way to put these developments in some sort of context, I sometimes imagine what my father would make of today's antiques industry. Many aspects of it would startle and perplex him. One would be the increase in the popularity of designers—my father never quite grasped how fundamental they would be to the antiques business. I think, too, he'd be happily astonished by the public's sophistication about antiques: in his day, people would come to Newel looking for an "antique cupboard"—now they're more likely to ask for a "Biedermeier armoire." By the same token, some furniture trends would strike him as odd: near the end of his life, people began moving away from glitzy, ormolu-ladened furniture toward simpler styles he didn't much value, for example, Art Deco or French '40s. And he'd be a little shocked, I think, by today's emphasis on credit. During his life, my father didn't even own a credit card—"I don't want to owe a dollar," he'd often say. Lastly, I don't believe he'd really grasp such new-fangled inventions as eBay—or the Internet as a whole.

But what would really astound my father—or rather, trouble him on a deep level—are the changes in the character of the modern antiques dealer. In his day, most dealers were born and bred into the field. Antiques were in their blood, their family trees, their genes. They were part of a family tradition whose expertise was very high. This tradition lives on among in such businesses as Florian Papp, Didier Aaron, Kentshire, Bernard Steinitz, French & Co. and others, but elsewhere, it is fading. Today—well, how can I put it? Too many people are entering the business just for the glamour of it without the proper knowledge or intuitive grasp of antiques. And this, in turn, undermines the public's confidence in our trade—a commodity more precious than a hundred *Normandie* panels.

Near the end of my own career, I began seeing at the London or Parisian shops examples of modern Yankee dealers buying anything they could grab without bothering to negotiate or even check the items' provenance.

Judgment is shockingly bad among many of these new dealers. I can't tell you how many times I've watched them engage in reckless buying that artificially drove up prices and in turn gave the public a false sense of the value of antiques. Knowledge is lacking, as well. Not too long ago, I went into an antiques store in downtown Manhattan and spotted some highly priced Art Deco commodes. I was stunned to find that the objects were reproductions not worth a fraction of their asking price. I questioned the dealer about the pieces, only to discover that he hadn't a clue that they weren't "right." I thought about alerting him, but I could see that nothing I'd say would change his opinion. Sadly, this was not the first incident, nor the last, in which I discovered that some of my younger colleagues were unknowingly offering reproductions as the real thing.

What can be done? First and foremost, people interested in the health of the antiques field must disseminate knowledge. Obviously, the more people know about antiques, the easier they will be able to detect the unknowledgeable—and unscrupulous—dealers from the true experts, and that can only help everyone in the field. But there are other steps the trade can take on its own to amend some business practices and bolster public confidence. I've already mentioned one—eliminating discounts. But there are one or two others.

Take price tags, for example. New York's Department of Consumer Affairs requires dealers to provide clear and accurate price tags on their antiques. And most of the established dealers are doing that, but there still remain many who don't. Instead of a simple dollar amount—like you might find in a department store—these dealers often mark their tags with a system of numbers or letters that secretly informs them what they paid for each object and for what they're willing to sell it. This information allows the dealer to raise or lower an object's price on the spot—a great advantage in negotiating with buyers. Unfortunately, buyers who know about this system can only feel annoyed, if not a little resentful. Now that you know about it, for example, will you ever be able to look at price tag in the same way? This is why I stress transparency in all transactions involving antiques—it's far more important than squeezing an extra buck out of a customer.

But perhaps the best, the most important, measure we can take to fulfill our obligation to the antiques buying public is to create an organization that examines the quality of the objects that dealers sell. In recent years, experts have been vetting the high-end antique fairs, why not institute a group that performs a similar function in high-end antique shops? Hired and funded by the trade itself, these antiques experts would certify that a dealer's objects are, in fact, authentic, and that he or she provides the public with clear, codeless price tags, along with other pertinent information about an antique, including the amount of restoration it contains. Dealers who meet these and other standards would receive a certificate to be visibly posted, assuring the public of the quality of their expertise and merchandise.

Impossible? Perhaps. A fantasy? Could be. Necessary? Absolutely. An organization entrusted with the task of vetting antiques shops would bolster public confidence by weeding out bad dealers—not only those who lack sufficient knowledge, but those who deliberately try to deceive the public. I can't tell you how disenchanted I felt when I recently visited the shop of a New York dealer to look at his French '40s furniture. There it was—an exquisite eight-foot iron dining room table created by the famous French designer Gilbert Poillerat, priced at a ridiculous level. But even at its exorbitant cost, the table might have tempted me—if it had been original. In truth, the "Poillerat" was a reproduction made a few years ago. Worse—much worse—the dealer knew exactly what he was doing. If enough of the antiques-buying public realized this deceit, it would certainly affect their confidence in our trade.

Given the growth, the glamorization and the diminishing connoisseurship in today's antiques trade, would I recommend that someone go into the antiques business? Only if he or she had the passion for the field *and* could inherit an existing business. Otherwise, I'd have to say no. My father established Newel with a table and twenty antiques—but that was in 1939. Today's basic business costs—rent, labor, advertising, and so on—would prohibit such humble beginnings. Moreover, largely because of the market muscle of interior designers, businesses today can no longer specialize, but have to provide a broad selection of antiques—and the investment it takes to create such holdings are also beyond the reach of most beginning dealers. And if the old-fashioned "specialist dealer" is out, so, too, is the collegial atmosphere they once enjoyed—nowadays, dealers are locked in fierce rivalry with one another, not to mention the auction houses. Once you combine these factors—business expenses, the need for a superb stock of antiques and the rough competition—you

can see the near impossibility these days of starting a high-end
antiques business from scratch. I don't want to discourage anyone
from trying, of course—heaven knows our field could use more
fresh, young talent—but you've got to be realistic about this sort
of thing.

In a real sense, the antiques trade is a victim of its own success. The boom we helped create caused prices to rise, auction
houses to flourish and increasing numbers of unknowledgeable
dealers and less-than-expert "experts" to flood the field. Meanwhile, the numbers of true dealers dwindle. A few families in
New York, London, and Paris are keeping the tradition alive, but
they're moving against current trends—and this, in turn, means
young people will find it harder to find the kind of mentors that
nurtured me and others of my generation. Perhaps this tendency
will reverse itself; we can only hope. Meanwhile, though, as the
over-all quality of the antiques trade diminishes, the notion of
caveat emptor becomes ever more pressing—as does the responsibility of the public to teach themselves about antiques. This is
one of the purposes of this book. I was fortunate to learn from
my father, plus years of hard experience. It's only right that I
share that knowledge with you. Which is why we will now direct
our attention away from dealers and designers to another area of
the trade you should know about: those oh-so-attractive palaces
of theater, money, and deceit that every antiques collector eventually enters—the auction house.

Chapter Fourteen

Reserves, Premiums, and Reforms

Webster's Collegiate Dictionary defines an auction as a "public sale of property to the highest bidder." Simple, right? Well, Christie's and Sotheby's want you to think so. They want you, as a member of the general public, to believe that within their imposing sales halls beautiful objects are sold in a simple, honest and transparent fashion. Now, anyone who's followed the news knows of the complicated, dishonest, and secretive manner in which these firms have operated—and how they paid the price for violating U.S. antitrust laws. But it might interest you to know that even before their monopolistic collusion over commission rates and other matters, Christie's and Sotheby's established an auction system that was—and still is—totally rigged, especially against buyers. You might be surprised to learn, for example, that the highest bidder frequently does not win the object, that auctioneers run up bids, take advantage of absentee bidders, disguise their vested interests in certain consignments and pull other shenanigans intended to manipulate the public. What's more, it's shocking that some of these business practices are perfectly legal.

The bottom line here? Behind their British accents and bold pinstripe suits, Christie's and Sotheby's hide a world of trickery and falsehood.

At the risk of repeating myself, let me state that I'm not a fan of the Big Two auction houses. However, I do admit that on rare occasions I've purchased items from them. And I acknowledge that their influence hasn't been totally bad: by captivating media attention with black tie auction "events," for example, they stimulated public interest in the fine and decorative arts. Moreover, both firms try hard (for their own commercial reasons, of course) to educate people about art and antiques through catalogues and lectures. And of course, there were many good, ethical people who worked at both companies. My friend John Marion is one, and so was the late, great Sotheby's auctioneer, Robert Woolley.

But as strong as these positives are, they do not balance the negatives. For over two decades, Christie's and Sotheby's have used their marketing and publicity machines to gain an unfair competitive advantage over the trade. By deliberately misrepresenting their business to the public, they racked up huge profits while taking business away from dealers. Worse, they created the illusion that they were the standards of connoisseurship and excellence in the trade—denigrating, in effect, the expertise we dealers had developed over years of hard work.

But the injustice of their prominence was what troubled me

the most. I disliked watching Christie's and Sotheby's gain power and influence through often devious means. These days, I take some solace knowing that their power and influence has diminished: it's hard to maintain your reputation when, like Sotheby's, you've payed tens of millions of dollars in fines, courts have sentenced Alfred Taubman, their former chairman, to jail and Diana "Dede" Brooks, their former CEO, to house arrest; or, like Christie's former chairman, Sir Anthony Tennant, can't step foot in the U.S. without getting arrested to face antitrust charges. But on the day-to-day level of auctions and consignment getting, the two houses continue their underhanded tactics. This has to stop. For the good of the antiques business, the public must become aware of the deceit that occurs at Christie's and Sotheby's—the sham beneath the glam, as it were. I can't tell you the whole story because of legal constraints—it would have to take something like an investigation by New York's attorney general Eliot Spitzer to reveal the whole truth. But I can give the outline of the problem so that hopefully you'll be forewarned—and forearmed.

Let's start at the beginning. Say you're interested in consigning an object—your grandmother's Georgian tea table, for example—for sale at Christie's or Sotheby's. (Much of what I'm going to say applies to smaller houses, as well, but since the Big Two set the standard for the entire auction industry, we'll focus on them.) In the course of arranging matters, you will sign a contract giving the house a fiduciary responsibility to act as your legal agent. In return for this service, the firm will levy, in addition to other fees, a seller's commission if the object is sold: this charge usually begins at ten percent. So far, so good. If they're going to sell granny's tea table for you, why shouldn't Christie's or Sotheby's take a cut? But this doesn't explain the "buyer's premium." This is also a commission, but one levied against the buyer, and it's a whopper: twenty percent at both Sotheby's and Christie's on the first $200,000 and twelve and a half percent on the rest. Now, *you're simply being penalized for buying.* These double commissions are more than greed—they are marks of desperation, and are in need of legal testing. I question whether the auctions can represent both buyer and seller without it being a conflict of interest. In their quest for auction material, Christie's and Sotheby's have, over the years, lowered consignor fees—sometimes waiving them altogether if they wanted something badly enough. In order to recoup this lost revenue, they've turned around and steadily raised their buyer's fees. (In part to stop competing over seller's commissions, Christie's and Sotheby's in the early 1990s agreed not to undercut each other's fees, a cozy agreement that led to federal antitrust investigations.) My point is that auction houses aren't transparent marketplaces. Like the waters of the North Atlantic, they hide icebergs everywhere.

At least the buyer's premium and seller's commission are public. The same can't be said of the "secret reserve." A fundamental part of the auction process, the secret reserve is so outrageous that politicians have tried to make it illegal. Yet it's still with us today, distorting the idea of a transparent sale. What is it? Well, a *reserve* is the minimum price a consignor will accept for an object sold at auction. It's a perfectly legal device, sanctioned by Rule 2-328 of the Uniform Commercial Code. But auction houses abuse it. How? By keeping the reserve confidential—or secret—and starting an auction at a value well below this amount. If no one in the room bids on the object, the auctioneer simply creates bids until the auction reaches the reserve. Confused? I'll take you through it, step by step.

Let's take that Georgian tea table again, but instead of consigning it to auction, you're interested in buying it. You check the catalogue and see that the table carries an estimate—or what the sales expert thinks it's worth—of $8,000–$10,000. Intrigued, you attend the auction, only to discover that when the table comes up for sale, the auctioneer starts the bidding at $4,000 (these figures, of course, are hypothetical). Hey, you think, I can get a bargain here, as you raise your paddle and bid $4,500. Suddenly, however, the bidding shoots to $7,500, even though you can't see another paddle in the room. What's going on? Whom are you bidding against? You may be bidding against no one. That's because the consignor has placed a reserve of $7,500 on the table. In order to goose the auction to that level, the auctioneer manufactures bids out of thin air—or from the "chandelier," which is why this ruse is called "chandelier bidding." They can run each object up to the consignor's secret reserve using make-believe bids, even if there are no bidders in the room.

Why don't auctioneers start the bidding at the object's reserve—in the case of the table, $7,500? Ah, but that would be too straightforward. By opening a sale at a level lower than a consignor's minimum price, an auctioneer hopes to mislead people into thinking as you did—that they can jump and snatch an object on the cheap. Moreover, with phantom bids, they can create the illusion of competition that may catch people up in "auction fever." That's why the houses don't publish reserves: if people knew each object's minimum price, they wouldn't raise their paddles until the bidding reached that level—and the entire auction would lack momentum and be over in twenty minutes. Is this trickery fair? Not in my book. Deceitful? Well, at the beginning of each auction, the auctioneer announces that he has the right to place bids "on behalf of the consignor"—a fancy way of saying he can create chandelier bids—but no one pays attention. Why aren't secret reserves and chandelier bids illegal? In the early 1990s, a New York State politician named Richard Brodsky attempted to pass legislation that would have outlawed them. At the time, Brodsky decried the practices as "fraudulent" and "deceptive"—a "theatrical game playing akin to pulling the wool over the consumer's eyes." But Christie's and Sotheby's hinted that laws preventing them from fooling the public might compel them to transfer the base of their operations to a more hospitable environment—London, for example, which would have cost New York City millions of dollars in sales tax. Politicians got worried and the legislation died. Perhaps they can run, but they can't hide. Recently an article in the British newspaper *Antiques Trade Gazette* quoted Robert Brooks, the Chairman of Bonhams (the third largest auction house), as saying "I still feel very strongly about the way we operate. We need to look at our industry and keep our houses in order. The auction industry hasn't had a smooth ride over the last five years. . . . We can't just take for granted that legislation isn't going to catch up with us." Quite an interesting observation, isn't it?

Reserves and chandelier bids are not the only things that you should be aware of when dealing with auction houses. If you check an auction catalogue, you'll find that the entries for certain objects include an obscure symbol indicating that the house has given each of those objects a guarantee. This means that the company has promised each consignor a set amount for his or her item, no matter how it performs at auction. And this means that the house has essentially purchased the object and now has a vested interest in its sale. So what, you say? Well, auction houses have numerous techniques to make one lot more enticing to the public than another: it can crank up the marketing machine to highlight this lot, display it more prominently in the catalogue, position it more advantageously in the order of the sale. When the object comes up on the block, the auctioneer can modulate his voice to increase audience interest in the piece (they are masters at this). The point is that once again, the auction houses are not the transparent markets that they claim to be—they have a whole system of smoke and mirrors designed to manipulate you, the buyer.

But if I'm selling an object, you ask, aren't the auction houses working in my interest? Yes and no. Obviously, secret reserves, chandelier bids, publicity blitzkriegs, subtle auctioneering tactics, and other techniques to increase bidding can help raise the hammer price of your consignment. But remember: there are a limited number of decorative arts auctions that occur each year, so you have to wait for your item to sell. Meanwhile, you must pay the house a slew of costs for shipping, photographing, insurance, and other services. Then comes the long-awaited auction—and your consignment fails to sell. Now what? You still owe the house a fee for handling the thing. But your problems may not end there. Objects that die at auction (the term is "buy in") are sometimes considered "burned"—that is, the market suspects that something is "not right" about them and these suspicions can make it harder for you to sell them in the future. Then there's the

matter of estimates: in order to obtain your consignment in the
first place, some auction house experts may tell you that it's
worth more than it really is. If the lot buys in, you not only owe
the auction house multiple fees, but you now must face the ig-
nominy of selling your antique at a level lower than the "experts"
claimed it was worth. And all the time you could have avoided
this *agita* by simply taking your piece to a friendly antiques
dealer.

This is why I advise you to contact one of my colleagues if
you want to sell an object. Along with what I've mentioned
above, you'll find that negotiations with dealers are far less com-
plex than wrangling with auction houses over estimates, insurance, catalogues fees, and so on. Dealers pay on the spot and pick
up the next day. These points are even more significant if you
want to buy antiques. Considering the number of galleries that
exist in any major city, dealers offer a better selection of material
than auction houses. Instead of the auction's high-pressure "bid
'n' buy" mentality, you can relax and take your time with dealers.
Most will even allow you to take an object home for awhile, just
to see if it agrees with your spouse, children, pets, living space,
etc. (Try that with an auction house!) Perhaps I'm prejudiced, but
I find that dealers are simply more knowledgeable about antiques
than most auction house experts.

To give you just one example, in 1999, the London *Sunday
Times* revealed that Sotheby's had been selling fake antiques for
years. This scandal first broke in 1997, when the senior specialist
of the English furniture department at Sotheby's London, Graham Child, resigned, in part over revelations that in 1994 he sold
a pair of fake Georgian chairs to a wealthy Canadian collector

Herbert Black for $730,000. (In 1996, Sotheby's sold a second pair of bogus Georgian chairs to an unknown buyer for a world record $1,300,000). Quoted at the time, Child said "people can get things wrong." Unfortunately, that wasn't the extent of the firm's mistakes, the *Times* noted. Despite numerous alerts from London dealers, Sotheby's sold such items as an eighteenth-century desk, a pair of George III painted jardinières, and a pair of Regency torchières—all of which turned out "not right." To give Sotheby's credit, the fakes, at least some of which originated from a London dealer, were well done; moreover, the firm eventually restituted buyers for the bad merchandise. But the issue in this particular case is not the honesty of the auction house, but its expertise. When the senior specialist in its furniture department, with twenty-one years of experience in the field, can't tell real from fake, what are we to think about the myriads of lower-level experts at both houses, some of whom have been in the business only a short time?

Still, I don't want to sound naïve about this topic. Nor do I want to appear unreasonable. There are times when something "to die for" comes up at Christie's and Sotheby's and you get that gotta have it feeling. In situations like that, I say, go ahead, register for your paddle and plunge into the fray. But please, listen to a few pieces of advice—especially if you're new to the game. There are more than icebergs in the auction waters—there are sharks, too. Sotheby's Web site may warn newcomers that *"caveat emptor is the coda of all auctions"*—but don't fall into their trap.

Let me walk you through a typical decorative arts auction, starting with the moment you open the catalogue. The first thing you notice are photographs of all the wonderful objects. But wait. Keep in mind that nothing in a catalogue looks the same in real life, no matter how well-photographed. Colors are off; the grain, texture and condition of materials is difficult to determine—and it's simply impossible to feel the essence, or "spirit" of top-quality antiques through photographs. Remember, too, that catalogues contain many innocent-looking words that are loaded with meaning: for example, an object dated as "twentieth-century" could be an original manufactured during the Edwardian Age, or a knock-off built three days before the Millennium. Similarly, the notation "Style," i.e., "Georgian style"—usually means that the object is a reproduction, as well. My point here—and this is very important—is never buy anything at auction that you don't actually see with your own eyes. Photographs, condition reports, descriptions from experts—these won't do. As with people, to truly love and cherish antiques, you have to meet them in person.

And this means attending the auction preview. Previews take place a week before a sale and offer you a chance to inspect the items scheduled to go on the block. They are also well designed to disguise the demerits of each piece. If you're willing to spend more than two or three thousand on an antique, seek out the expert in charge of the sale and pepper him or her with questions. Don't be intimidated. Remember, they want your money. They want it badly.

Ask about condition. How much repair does the piece need? Has it been restored? If it's a chair, check its arms and legs—are they sturdy? Examine the springs for tautness. If you're dealing with a cabinet, inspect its hinges—are they tight? Are the shelves original, what do the drawers look like? If the object seems uneven, is it because of age, or the way the porters assembled it? Look for wormholes. If you find any, tap the piece—if dust emerges from the hole, chances are the worm is still living inside. And don't forget to ask the porters to turn the object over, so you can inspect the underside of the piece. You never know: that $1 million Goddard-Townsend commode you've fallen in love with may very well hide a reproduction leg in the back.

But while you're "kicking the tires," don't look too interested. I know this sounds silly, considering all the trouble you're going through to inspect the object. But you never want to reveal too much information to auction personnel, especially if you're interested in an expensive piece. If the house thinks you're eager to buy, sales personnel will often do their best to grease your wallet through flattering attention, compliments and other chitchat. But that's nothing compared to what they'll do during the auction. The auctioneer will know where you're sitting (that's his business, after all), and when your piece comes up for sale, he will look you directly in your eye to get you to bid. On paper, that doesn't sound like much. In real life, surrounded by the glitz and glamour of the sale, it can be intimidating. I remember once bidding on an object, and when the level surpassed my limit, I stopped—at which point the auctioneer stared at me, shook his head, and said "I don't believe it." I held fast, but I'll tell you, a part of me didn't want to disappoint the guy and I almost threw in just one more bid. If I felt pressured, how much more so will someone not familiar with auctions?

But I'm getting ahead of myself. For your pre-sale examination is not yet complete. An hour or two before the event, make sure you take one more look at the piece. Why? To see what happened since you saw it last: after all, porters have moved the antique several times, perhaps jarring, banging or otherwise damaging it in some way.

Finally, though, the sale arrives. For drama's sake, let's imagine we're at a high-end decorative arts auction, lots of outstanding Biedermeir and superb Art Deco material, the smell of perfume and money is intermingling with the lights and buzz of the salesroom, and you're planning on dropping a considerable amount of money. You're tense, adrenalin's flowing—you figure others want the piece too and you anticipate a bidding war. Relax. Get control of your emotions, settle in your seat, and remind yourself not to get caught up in bidding fever. Like gambling casinos, auction houses love the customer who hurls caution to the wind. Set a price limit and stick to it. But keep in mind, too, that if the object is really good, and you really want it, you're going to have to pay.

Position yourself in the rear of the salesroom. Why? That way you can get an overall perspective of the sale—you're observing your environment as much as participating in it. Now comes the low rumble of machinery, your beautiful antique swivels out on the carousel from backstage, the auctioneer in his fine-timbered English accent says, "I have here now a magnificent example of—" and he starts the bidding. And you plunge right in to show everyone that you're a determined buyer, right? Wrong. Remember the secret reserve! The price is going to rise even if no one waves a paddle, so don't do the auctioneer's work for him. Let him pull bids out of the chandelier for awhile.

When you think it's down to one or two bidders, then raise your paddle. A new player leaping in at the last moment can demoralize your competition. And should your rival offer another bid, snap back a crisp, authoritative counter bid. You might even jump an increment: if the auctioneer raises each level by $500, take it up $1,000. Let the room know you mean business. you've money to burn (hey, this is theater, remember?), you want that object, no matter what.

Do not, however, raise your paddle and keep it there, *à la* the Statue of Liberty. Some auction goers do this (it's called "lighthouse bidding"), thinking that it signals to other buyers back off, I'm getting this thing and I don't care what it costs. But you're more likely to get bid up by people seeking to test your resolve. My advice—and I extend this to every aspect of the auction process—is never reveal your intentions until the last possible moment.

What if you can't attend the auction? Should you put in an "absentee bid?" I caution against it. Auctioneers will sometimes look at someone's pre-registered bid and start the sale at that amount. I learned this lesson very early in my career when I was on a buying trip to London and didn't want to spare the time to attend a sale in person. I left a bid for £6,000 for a pair of chairs, and later discovered that the auctioneer had opened the sale at that amount. No one else bid, and I bought the objects. The problem was, if the auctioneer had started the sale at the reserve, or lower, I might have purchased the chairs at a lesser amount. Can I prove deceit? No. But I'm not the only one who's noticed this auctioneering trick. This is why I tell people who can't attend an auction to do their bidding by phone. It's not difficult: you make arrangements with the auction house to have an employee stationed in the salesroom call you a few lots before your object comes up on the block; then, when your item does come up, you instruct the employee when to bid. This way, not only are you "present" in the room, but you may bluff your competition into folding. For all they know, that phone bidder they're vying against is an Arabian sheik with pockets as deep as an oil well.

Inevitably, if you attend enough auctions, you'll get beat on an item or two. What should you do then? First, congratulate yourself on not getting swept away by auction fever. Then, console yourself with the thought that I always used to ease the sting of defeat: you were not "meant" to own that antique. It's a different matter, however, if the object you wanted "passed"—or failed to sell. In that case, call the department head the following day and mention that you'd like to make a reasonable offer for the lot, and could he or she contact the consignor? By "reasonable" I mean an offer below the lowest bid the object received at the sale. Since many of the consignments originate from dealers, chances are the owner will be eager to sell. You'll be surprised at how well this works.

I could go on. But I'm afraid of overloading you with advice. Besides, no matter how much someone tells you about an auction, there's no substitute for the actual experience of standing on the salesroom floor, paddle in hand, ready for battle. Like bungee jumping or crocodile wrestling, it's an adventure. And if, like many status-conscious Baby Boomers, you think that throwing your money around in a fashionable media event is a shortcut to class and status, these events are for you. I always preferred hunting for antiques in quiet, hidden places of the world, where the rewards were the beauty of undiscovered treasures, rather than the evanescent glitz of public attention.

Still, it was always a problem for me what to do about the trickery that I saw at the auction firms. I couldn't very well walk up and down York Avenue or Rockefeller Center passing out accusatory flyers. A few years ago, just as the Christie's–Sotheby's collusion scandal broke, I tried to interest some of my fellow dealers in running a full-page ad in the *New York Times.* It showed an image of a stern looking woman holding a paddle, below a caption reading:

JUDGING BY SOME AUCTION HOUSES' BEHAVIOR,
PERHAPS THERE'S ANOTHER USE FOR THEIR PADDLES

followed by a paragraph informing the public that "there are dealers who have served the public for many generations offering authenticated antiques at prices that are fair and fully stated with no hidden reserves or buyer's premium." But I decided that despite my objections to the misbehavior of the auction houses, it would be wrong to hit them when they were down. I abandoned the idea.

In the end, though, it didn't really matter. With the antitrust investigations, Christie's and Sotheby's received their comeuppance, and dealers have reclaimed much of the moral high ground they've traditionally occupied. But more importantly, rather than a single advertisement, my whole career at Newel had been a challenge—or at least an alternative—to the auction houses. I built up a comprehensive inventory of material to rival the supermarket atmosphere they offer to the public. I took the Big Two on at their own marketing game, spending millions of dollars in attractive magazine ads. I cultivated editors, reporters and other journalists. I became the spokesman for one of the

largest banks in the nation. I wasn't shy at promoting myself or
Newel or the trade—but I had to; Christie's and Sotheby's were
stiff competition. And I'm proud to say that I gave as good as I
got, and despite the rough-and-tumble aspects of the antiques
trade, that not a breath of scandal ever attached itself to the company my father established in a Second Avenue storefront sixty-
six years ago.

It seems like yesterday—but at the same time, ages ago. Like
my father in his own day, I am struck with a bittersweet realization that my era in the antiques trade has come to an end. Years
pass, taste and people change. Looking back, I see that I caught a
wave of excitement in antiques that began with the establishment
of Newel, accelerated with Peter Wilson and Jackie, then crested
just before the auction house scandals. Now, it's tapering off. With
so many antiques around, buyers concentrate mostly on top-quality material, ignoring second- and third-rate stuff. Prices are still
rising—as with real estate, the value of top quality antiques will
always rise—but much of the excitement and glamour of the
trade is gone. It will return, of course: a new generation of buyers, excited by what they see on the Internet or some other new
technology will rediscover the objects of the past and begin buying again. Eventually, every generation discovers the glories of
what came before them.

I was fortunate to discover these glories at an early age. No
other profession would have given me the opportunity to experience such magic and beauty—from a humble dining room chair
to the *Normandie* panels and my beloved Fantasy Furniture. What
more can a person ask for? My life has been enriched beyond all
measure by the antiques I've nurtured. Each day I entered Newel,

I looked forward to another day of work, a day spent learning about the objects of history, and how they influence our lives, our thoughts, our imaginations.

Occasionally, standing by the grave of my father, it dawns on me that I succeeded in doing what he'd always instructed—I didn't come back until I had found it. By that I mean, I've managed to find meaning to the brief span of years God granted me on this planet. This meaning came mostly through my family, of course, always my greatest joy. But I also gleaned something from the course of history: how, together with my father, I formed part of that great twentieth-century saga known as the American Dream. And how, through Newel, I served as a caretaker for the objects that adorned the lives of people who lived in even earlier times, how, in a very real way, I helped bring their existence into our own era. A person finds fulfillment by connecting with a force larger than his own existence. Through antiques, I have touched the mystery of time.

I hope you've gained something from my adventures in the antiques trade. As I mentioned at the start of this book, fifty years ago, my father brought me to Newel to wax and clean, dust and polish antiques. Today, after a lifetime in the business, I find that, in my mind, I'm still that little boy, still wandering the aisles of the shop, waxing and cleaning, dusting and polishing the objects I love. It's been my life, it's where part of me will always be, along with my immediate family. I can't imagine anything better.

Index

A

Aaron, Didier 200
Abrams, Harry N. (publisher) 140
Ackroyd, Dan 104
Addams Family Values (movie) 105
Adweek 78
All My Children (television show) 36
Allen, Woody 105, 107
Alma-Tadema, Lawrence 101
Angel Street (play) 31
Antiques Roadshow, The (televison show) 19
Antiques Trade Gazette 210
Architectural Digest 67, 74, 76, 77, 80, 81, 139
Art Director's Club 78
Astaire, Fred 108
Astoria Studio 23
Atlantic City 55, 56
Aubusson 124
Aurora (Roman goddess) 124

B

Baer, Lewis 29, 68, 70–71, 82, 84–85
Baker, Josephine 124
Baldwin, Alec 104
Baldwin, Billy 3, 66, 194
Baloun, Philip 80, 143
Bancroft, Anne 97
Bank of North America 72
Bara, Theda 23
Bass, Sid 116

Bastille 120
Bath (English city) 172
Beaton, Cecil 109, 110
Ben-Hur (movie) 25
Bennet, James 10
Benoits (Family) 119–127
Berenson, Bernard 25, 67
Bergdorf-Goodman 74
Beverly (*See* Beverly Mendel)
Black, Herbert 212
Blake, William 135
Bonhams (auction house) 210
Bourne, Mel 106, 111
Boxer, Leonard 73
Boyer, Charles 108
Brando, Marlon 112
Brandus, Judith (*See* Judith
    Newman)
Brighton Pavilion 45, 46, 50, 53, 65, 82,
    133, 136, 137, 139, 144, 148, 156, 166,
    172
Brodsky, Richard 210
Brooklyn Dodgers 37
Brooklyn Museum of Art (BMA) 39, 40,
    41, 141, 142
Brooks, Diana "Dede" 207
Brooks, Mel 97
Brooks, Robert 210
Buatta, Mario 66, 84, 143, 194
Buck, Robert 40, 141, 143, 147
Bugatti, Carlo 136

Bulow, Claus von 111
Burns & Co. 23–24, 27, 30, 81
Burton, Richard 80
Bush, George 198

C

Camden Passage 173
Camelot (play) 108
Candid Camera (television show) 100, 101
Carnegie Museum of Art 131
Castille (hotel) 169, 170, 172
Central Synagogue 80
Chanel, Coco 110–111
Channel 13 (New York) 83
Chapanais 141
Chemical Bank 83, 143
Chester, Hilda 37
Child, Graham 212
Christie's (auction house) 19, 67, 75, 76, 98, 129, 139, 166, 205, 206, 207, 208, 210, 213, 219, 220
Christolfe 124
Citizen Kane (movie) 121
Clarendon Court 111, 112
Cleopatra (movie) 25
Clignancourt 121
Clinton White House 10
Coco (play) 110
Colt, Alvin 57, 62
Compagnie Général Transatlantique 125
Condé Nast (publisher) 140
Coney Island 23
Connoisseur (magazine) 70, 82, 83, 84, 86, 128, 129, 175, 182
Cooper Union 26, 43
Cooper, Peter 26
Coopers & Lybrand 70
Coppola, Francis Ford 112
Cotswolds 172, 177
Coward, Noel 108
Creveling, Joanne 159
Crosby, Bing 91

D

Daily Express (newspaper) 160

Dali, Salvador 124
Daum Brothers 124
David Linley Furniture, Ltd. 157
Dawn, the Four Winds, and the Sea (mural) 124
Days of Wine and Roses (movie) 75
Deisroth, Barbara 97
Department of Consumer Affairs 201
deMille, Cecil B. 80
Dietrich, Marlene 2, 38, 124
Diller, Barry 112
Dixon, Donna 104
Dobkin, John 142
Domus (magazine) 43
Doyle, Sarah Jackson 114
Dunand, Jean 125, 129
Duncan, Alastair 129, 140
Dupas, Jean 125, 129
Duveen, Joseph 25, 67, 108, 182, 183, 198

E

Eames, Charles 43
Eames, Ray 43
eBay 19, 178, 194, 200
Ebbets Field 37
Edison, Thomas 23
Edward VII 145
Eisenhower, David 114
Eisenhower, Dwight 48
Eisenhower, Julie 114
Eisenhower, Mamie 48
Eisner, Michael 104
Elio's (restaurant) 113
Elizavetgrad (Russian town) 22
Ellis Island 21–22
Erté 140, 143
Extraordinary Furniture (book) 152, 154, 158, 159, 162

F

"Fantasy Furniture" (exhibition) 7, 40–41, 82–83, 133–149, 151
Fantasy Furniture (book) 134, 140–141, 145, 150–162
Fairbanks, Douglas, Jr. 23

Field of Dreams (movie) 72
Fine Arts Committee (White House) 3, 9
Flammarion (publisher) 140
Fleming, Ian 51
Fonda, Jane 4, 80, 97
Forbes (magazine) 85
Forbes, Christopher "Kip" 129, 143
Forbes, Malcolm 96, 116
Fort Dix 47, 48
42nd Street (play) 79
Four Horseman of the Apocalypse (movie) 25
Fox, Michael J. 104
Frank, Jean-Michel 92
Franklin, Alan 172
French & Co. 200
Frick, Henry 108
Fulham Road 173, 174
Funt, Alan 100
Funt, Marilyn 100

G

Gable, Clark 42
Gallagher, Mary 8
Gallé, Émile 136
Gambler, The (movie) 103
Garbo, Greta 2, 35
Garland, Judy 91
Gaudí, Antonio 135
Gershwin, Ira 157
Godfather I (movie) 112
Godfather II (movie) 112
Goldberg, Sam 20, 32
Goldschmidt Collection 51
Goodman, Benny 90
Gould (Florence) Foundation 131
Grand Salon *(Normandie)* 7, 118, 124, 125
Grant, Cary 124
Grauman's Chinese Theatre 25
Greene, Belle 67
Greenspan, Nolan 85
Greenspan, Phoebe 85
Greenspan, Teddy 85
Greenspan, Emily 20, 55, 84–85, 116, 133, 138, 149
Guccione, Bob 80, 115

Guimard, Hector 93, 145
Guys and Dolls (play) 108

H

Hadley, Albert 66
Hampton, Mark 66, 84, 104, 143, 198
Harrison, Rex 80, 109, 143
Hayward, Brooke 112
Hearst, Randolph 116
Hearst, Veronia 143
Hearst, William Randolph 108
Hellman, Lillian 52, 90
Hemion, Dwight 91
Hepburn, Katharine 2, 36
Hertz Corporation 49
Hill, Clint 3, 4, 8
Hillman (Henry L. Foundation) 131
Hoffman, Dustin 107–108
Horn, Steve 76
House & Garden (magazine) 67, 74, 80, 141, 152
Hoving, Thomas 82–83, 128, 140, 143, 146
Hullabaloo (television show) 91
Hunt, Lamar 116
Hunzinger, George 40

I

Ile de France (ship) 124, 125
Interiors (movie) 105, 107
Intolerance (movie) 25
Isabell, Robert 80

J

J. Walter Thompson (ad agency) 78
Jackson, Michael 116, 167
Janjigian, Robert 140
Janniot, Alfred Auguste 124
Jouve, Georges 124
"Judge Judy" (Sheindlin, Judith) 85

K

Kantor, Evelyn (*See* Evelyn Newman)
Kaufman, George S. 52
Kaufmann, William III 78
Kempner, Nan 143
Kennedy, Jackie 1–11, 51, 67, 80, 86, 89, 90,

Kennedy, Jackie *(continued)*
    92, 148, 193, 194, 198, 220
Kennedy, Ruth 157
Kenneth, Mr. 2
Kensington Church Street 173
Kentshire 200
Ketcham, James 9
Kilgallen, Dorothy 35–37
King and I, The (play) 31
King George IV (*See* Prince of Wales)
Kings Road 173
Kirovograd (*See* Elizavetgrad)
Kissinger, Henry 85, 198
Koch, Frederick R. 132
Kollmar, Richard 35–37
Kravis, Henry 139, 198

L

La Cage aux Folles (play) 31
Landau, Marilyn 27, 55, 56, 63, 64, 65, 68,
    69, 70, 100
Lake Tarleton Club 49
Lalique, René 124
Lamm, Richard 10
Lasser, Louise 107
Lauder, Estée 198
Lauder, Mrs. Ronald 143
Lauren, Ralph 116
Lavagetto, Cookie 36
Le Corbusier 43
Leach, Robin 25, 83
Lee, Gypsy Rose 2
Le Havre 124
Lehman, Arnold 40, 142
Leleu, Jules 92, 124
Lemmon, Jack 72
Lerman, Leo 140
Lewis (*See* Lewis Baer)
Liberace 110, 111
Life (magazine) 37
Lifestyles of the Rich and Famous 25, 83
Lincoln Bedroom (White House) |
    10–11
Linley, Viscount David 151–162
Lois, George 76
Lord Pengo (play) 108

Loring, John 112, 140
Louvre Des Antiquaires 97, 121

M

Macklowe, Harry 73
Maine Antiques Digest 157
Males, Mildred 71, 89, 93
Manning, Burt 78
Marcus, Stanley 116, 140
Marilyn (*See* Marilyn Landau)
Marion, John 76, 140, 182, 206
Marks Ellis 30, 35–36, 41, 43, 52, 57, 61, 68,
    69–71, 81, 86, 148
Marron, Catie 143
McCartney, Paul 91
McEnroe, John 98
McGuire, Al 43
McQueen, Steve 48
Mellon, Andrew 108
Mendel, Beverly 27, 55, 56, 63, 64, 65, 66,
    69, 70
Metropolitan Museum of Art 80, 82, 128,
    140
Metzger, Robert 98, 143
Minnelli, Liza 91
Miss K (*See* Evelyn Newman)
Mt. Carmel Cemetery 60, 85
My Fair Lady (play) 109

N

National Academy of Design 40, 82, 134,
    142–148
National Endowment for the Arts 131
Newman, Evelyn 35, 36, 39, 52, 63
Newman, Judith 9, 10, 20, 41, 49–56, 69,
    74, 77, 84, 85, 100, 113, 130, 138, 149,
    160, 161, 166
Newman (Judith and Bruce) Gallery
    40
New York Magazine 158, 160
New York Post 160
New York Times 10, 80, 82, 141, 147, 219
Newman, Meyer 21, 22–32, 38, 39, 42, 50,
    53, 55, 59, 60, 63, 81
Nichols, Mike 109
Niven, Fernanda 143

Nixon, Pat 114
Nixon, Richard 113, 115
Nixon, Tricia (Mrs. Edward Cox) 80, 114, 115
Normandie (ship) 7, 63, 79, 117–132, 139, 149, 151, 200, 220

O

O'Neil, Tatum 98
Olnick, Bob 73
Ono, Yoko 4, 116
Owen, Mickey 37

P

Painter, Raymond 174
Paley, Babe 113
Papp, Florian 200
Paramount Studios 23, 112
Paris Opera 120
Park Avenue Armory 139
Pearl Harbor 125
Penthouse (magazine) 115
Pepper, Eleanor 44
Perry Como Show (televison show) 91
Petrie, Carroll 143
Petrie, Milton 143
Philco Television Playhouse (televison show) 36
Picasso, Paloma 80, 110
Pilgrim, Diane 141
Pimlico Road 152, 159, 173
Pitts, Zasu 90
Playhouse 90 (television show) 36
Polo (store) 26, 74
Portobello Road 75, 173
Pratt Institute 43, 44, 47, 51, 72, 76, 80, 82, 141, 148, 160
Prince Regent (Prince of Wales, later King George IV) 46, 47, 53, 136
Prince, Hal 116
Princess Margaret 152
Private Lives (play) 80, 112

R

Radziwill, Lee 80, 113. 143
Rense, Paige 81

Rhoem, Carolyn 198
Riva, William 38
Rive Gauche (Paris) 170, 171
Rizzoli Publications 140, 159
Rockefeller, John D. 108
Rogers, Kenny 97, 103
Rose, Billy 52
Ross, Wilbur 142
Rothschild, Guy de 80
Rudnick, Paul 105
Ruhlmann, Jacques Emil 92, 124

S

St. John's University 43, 72
Saint Quen 75
Saks Fith Avenue 74
San Simeon 46
Sarnoff, Mrs. William 143
Saturday Night Live (televison show) 36
Scaife Gallery 131
Schalit, Gene 141
Schmied, François-Louis 124
Schwartz, Marvin 140
Sinatra, Frank 91
Sirowitz, Len 76
Sister Parish 66, 75, 140
Sloan (Matthew Scott) Collection 41
Smith, Gary 91
Smith, Oliver 9, 107–109
Snowdon, Lord 152
Sotheby's (auction house) 5, 19, 51, 67, 75, 76, 97, 98, 101, 111, 139, 140, 166, 182, 205, 206, 207, 208, 210, 212, 213, 219, 220
Sound of Music (play) 31, 108
Spanierman Gallery 53
Steinberg, Saul 80, 198
Steinitz, Bernard 170, 200
Stewart, Jimmy 124
Stewart, Rod 97
Streisand, Barbra 4, 80, 89–93, 96, 193
Subes, Raymond 124
Suffern-Tailer, Jean 143

T

Taubman, Alfred 207

Taylor, Elizabeth 80, 112
Tea and Sympathy (play) 31
Temple of Dendur 80
Thief of Baghdad (movie) 25
Thompson, James 113
Thomspon, Jayne 113
Tiffany & Company 112, 140
Time (magazine) 141
Tisch, Jonathan 80
Today Show (television show) 141
Todd, Mike 2
Trauffer, F. Peter 136
Trump, Ivana 113
Tudor, W. Pendleton 78
Turner, Ted 97

V

Valentino, Rudolph 23
Versailles (palace) 125
Vogue Décoration (magazine) 147

W

Wallace, Mike 198
Walters, Barbara 116

Warhol, Andy 105
Weaver, Sigourney 98–100
West Side Story (play) 108
Westboune Grove 173
What's My Line? (television show) 35
Williams, Solveig 159
Wilson, Peter 51, 66, 76, 83, 90, 193, 220
Winfrey, Oprah 113
Woolley, Robert 76, 206
Working Girl (movie) 98–99
Wright, Craig 104
Wright, Frank Lloyd 113
Wrightsman, Jayne 3

Y

Your Show of Shows (television show) 36

Z

Zipkin, Jerome 143
Zwiebel, Alan 78